THE LITTLE BOOK

OF AMAZING

BUSINESS STORIES

Edited by
Sue Wybrow

Contributors
Monir Ali, Neil Barras-Smith, Catherine Batour,
Kim Bradford, Louise Brennan, Julie Brian, Emma Bustamante,
Liz & Tommy Carey, Steve Clarke, June Cory, Matt Dawson,
Amanda Dilworth, Danielle Durant, Ruth Farenga, Jenny Ford,
Christine Frith, Jo Hailey, Susan Heaton-Wright, Lucy Holliday,
Nikki Howes, David Jenkins, Hannah Knight, Sarah Lomax,
Cheryl Luzet, Adarsh Mehta, Toula & James Messer, Suzy
Moody, Eileen Morrison, Louise Murphy, Marian Murphy, Donna
Nichol, Nicky Packman, Aarti Parmar, Ben Schneider, James
Sheehan, Sally Shepherd, Kristina Snarskiene, Jenny Soppet-
Smith, Debbie Stewart, Clare Suttie, Deborah Temple, Christo
Tofalli, Gill Turton, Nicky Weisfeld, Ian & Melanie Wooding-
Jones, Sarah Wren, Sue Wybrow

Published by
The Endless Bookcase Ltd.
71 Castle Road, St Albans, Hertfordshire, England, AL1 5DQ.
www.theendlessbookcase.com

Printed in the United Kingdom
Also available in multiple e-book formats.
First published in 2017.

ISBN: 978-1-912243-18-1

This book is dedicated to all the passionate, brave and determined people who go for it and follow their dreams - you rock!

Ooh and to all our families and friends who support and encourage us on our roller coaster rides.

WHY THIS BOOK?

From starting St Albans Business jellies (co-working events) a fair few years ago, to the Facebook group which at the time of writing has over 3,000 businesses in St Albans within it - I've seen a massive difference to many business owners as well as their businesses.

From start ups thinking that they weren't real "business people", to those drinking in tons of information and feeling totally overwhelmed, to people turning their "hobby" into a business - one thing was clear to see - the drive, determination, comradery, support and help these amazing people had and were willing to give each other.

The growth of many of those businesses has been incredible, the difference in those individuals has been amazing, the confidence, strength, belief and passion absolutely incredible.

We want to share these stories with YOU - to share with you that "normal" people can make it happen - that you can follow your dreams and achieve them - whatever they may be.

And my favourite quote of all time "Life moves pretty fast. If you don't stop and look around once in a while you could miss it" - by the fabulous Ferris Bueller! Don't miss life - follow your dreams and go for it!

Sue Wybrow - Chief Legwarmer Wearer - Popdance World

FOREWORD

Home Start HERTFORDSHIRE
Support and friendship for families

Home Start

£1 from each sale of this book goes to Home Start Hertfordshire - from a chance conversation at the St Albans Businesses Jelly to say that Home Start had had their funding cut - and St Albans Businesses (SAB) were looking for a local charity to support - a great relationship was formed.

From "Naked" Christmas Cards to a fantastic Justin Timberlake spoof video, SABs have raised thousands of pounds for Home Start.

Suzy Moody explains: Home Start helps give children the best possible start in life by supporting parents as they grow in confidence, build resilience and find ways to manage the challenges they face. We want parents to feel that they are being the best parent they can be.

We know that a nurturing, stable family life teaches our children how to love, how to learn and paves the way to a happy, confident adulthood, but being at breaking point means even the smallest tasks are overwhelming – bedtime stories, making dinner and sometimes, even just getting up each morning!

Home Start volunteers visit families at home each week, supporting parents who are facing challenges such as isolation, bereavement, multiple births, illness, disability or who are just finding parenting a struggle.

They build trusted and non-judgemental relationships and support the individual needs of the family in a way that no other service does.

So thank you for buying this book because it is not just a book; this is you helping Home-Start turn fragile families into strong families, enable vulnerable children to become safe and happy children; you are investing in the future of our community.

www.home-startherts.org.uk

Steve Clarke

Entrepreneur, inspirational speaker, business mentor and specialist in the field of sales and marketing. Author, of "How to thrive... not just survive" and a regular columnist for numerous publications.

It's all about attitude... and action

So here I sit, working on my iPad via the internet on the rooftop terrace of the Kimpton Canary Hotel in Santa Barbara, California fleshing out another simple business plan. To my left, bathed in sunshine, the beautiful backdrop of the majestic Santa Ynes mountains, to my right the glistening Pacific Ocean all set under clear blue skies, I'm wondering; what could possibly go wrong as I'm about to embark upon yet another entrepreneurial journey....

It feels like a far cry from my early business career, working out of a small shop on Victoria Street, St Albans selling office stationery, but is it?

Geographically, hell yes! In practical terms... not in the least bit.

This book is packed with real life stories from real life entrepreneurs. I hope you'll find them inspiring. I hope you can draw useful and practical lessons from each one of them. I also hope you can find the time to pat a few of them on the back and say well done and maybe even offer some encouragement to those just starting out too.

Maybe just maybe, something within these pages will be that catalyst that sets you off on your own exciting roller coaster ride of self-employment!

A good friend of mine, former Olympian turned TV personality and motivational speaker Kriss Akabussi once told me this; role models should not be looked up to, they should be looked into.

It's so true. So as you read each persons' account of their challenges, their successes, their ups and their downs, see if you can see which lessons translate into your world. Look into what makes them tick, what drives them... what's their "why"?

This is what you must lock into if you are to succeed in your own business. You must know your 'why'. You will need to remind yourself on the dark, cold winters morning "why" you're doing this.

You need a bulletproof emotional connection to what you are doing and know "why" failure is not an option... You should be able to visualise the end product and know "why" you have to

Succeed...

From all the business people I've met, there's a common thread woven into the very fabric of every successful "entrepreneur".

Irrespective of the industry or sector, there are just a few things in truth;

Vision, purpose, belief and action.

Be crystal clear on your vision. Where are you going? What are you creating?

Know your purpose. Why are you doing what you are doing... and it's not all about the money.

Create an unshakable belief in yourself, your products or your services.

Finally, once you adopt the right attitude - it's all about action.

My life is set to take yet another twist and turn, such is the life of an entrepreneur. Since my early days of selling office stationery in St Albans, I've tried my hand at many things - not all screaming successes, but I tried. I had a vision, I took action. In hindsight, perhaps on one or two ventures the purpose and belief were missing or not strong enough.

Amongst the twists and turns, I've started a ski business in the USA which I floated on the stock market. Started an IT company in Harlow which I grew to £32m a year before selling that on. For several years I've had a successful career as an international professional speaker and business mentor. In the last couple of months I've just created and launched the worlds' first Bluetooth lapel mic and companion app for use with a smartphone, www.LoveHeyMic.com... and now - I'm about to turn my world upside down once more and move to California as I set up www.advantage.net.

This time I'm going to disrupt the trucking industry with a revolutionary piece of 'clean tech' that reduces fuel consumption by 25% and emissions by 35%... Vision, purpose, belief and action all locked down... wish me luck, I'm going in...

I wish you every success on your journey.

It's all about attitude and action - best of luck.

Steve Clarke

www.eurekaselling.co.uk
www.loveheymic.com
www.addvantage.net

CONTENTS

NICKY WEISFELD
Valuing Minds

I've run a business before – a successful business, a multi-million pound business, a medium sized enterprise employing quite a few people – and with a business partner that I'd known and worked with for years. But this time, it's just me (well, at the moment anyway).

So, if it succeeds or fails, it's down to me. A bit daunting really – no one I can blame if things go wrong. No one I can rely on to bring in work. No one to do the strategy, marketing, sales, paperwork, books, delivery and so on. Just me!

So why on earth would I put myself in this potentially risky position? To start with, it was boredom. Having worked as a psychologist for most of my adult life (both in education and then business) and having sold the company, I took some time out and then did various roles helping friends who had businesses of their own – a touch of change management here, some bookkeeping there and masses of admin. But I could feel my brain atrophying with each load of filing and I was BORED.

I decided to go back to the thing that I had trained for all those years ago, Educational Psychology, as it would require the little grey cells to be working steadily, if not on overtime.

Having been out of the profession for over 20 years (though I had worked as a Business Psychologist for much of that time), I knew I would have to jump through various hoops to regain my registration with the Health and Care Professions Council (HCPC).

The hoops amounted to 60 days in a 12-month period, made up of supervised work, attending courses and events, and private study. The last two of these were easy – I booked myself onto courses and workshops. I read heavy tomes on psychology and education that worked better than any pills at sending me to sleep. I met up with former colleagues and picked their brains, relieved to hear that many of the issues and approaches I had used years before were still around, although the acronyms had changed a bit, and multiplied.

But the supervision was a problem. Local Authority Psychologists were already involved in supervising trainees. The private psychologists didn't want to know; maybe they saw me as future competition. In any event, having racked up numerous days and still not found a supervisor, 12 months had passed, so all the stuff I had done at the start began to fall out of the time period.

Eventually, I found a sympathetic ed psych who agreed to supervise me and I started doing work with and for him – for a fee! Fast forward twelve months and I put my forms into the HCPC for re-registration.

Rejection number 1 came because I hadn't read the small print properly: no more than half the 60 days could come from private study. So, I did more supervised work and went on more courses. Bear in mind that all this was costing me, so I was building up expenses even before the business had started. And, as time passed, more things fell outside the start of the crucial 12-month period.

Rejection number 2 in June 2016 was because I was using an old form I had previously downloaded so the registration fee was wrong. Rather than just ring and ask for the difference, the whole thing was cancelled and sent back.

Rejection number 3 followed in July (something to do with the type of application), but in September, success! I was on my way.

Having worked in local authorities many moons ago, I decided to work independently this time and had several ideas about how I wanted to proceed. I had come up with a business name but found that there was an Australian Ed Psych practice using the same name (though they didn't own the .com domain name). As a matter of courtesy, I sent them an email saying I would be launching in the UK with the name and they threatened me with a lawsuit as they were selling resources globally. Back to square one.

Fortuitously, it was around this time that I went to my first St Albans Businesses (SAB) jelly and had the great fortune to sit at a table with Digital Jen and Cobbled Kitchen Danielle. Within two hours, I had my business name, my domain name and several variants of it were registered and we'd started planning the website. Jenny introduced me to Aarti and that led to my brand design, which I love – and which is totally different to others working in my space.

The business started October 1st and after a frenetic period of setting processes and systems up, purchasing the kit I needed and writing, the website went live in November. One of the things I did early on was join all the relevant associations and databases I could. And two days after the website went live, I had my first client!

Thankfully they keep coming, even with little active marketing. The cases are always interesting, sometimes challenging, and with these and the lecturing work I do, I'm happily in profit each month. I should make a small profit this year despite all the start-up costs and having to take some time out of the business twice this year (one of the perils of working for yourself).

Has it been worth it? Most definitely! Not only am I thinking again, which makes me feel good, but I am getting good feedback and am providing practical help and advice to parents and children about their education. I like feeling in control of what I'm doing – I can accept or turn away cases (as I have done when I felt it was outside my expertise) – and doing as much (or as little) work as I want.

My family have been incredibly supportive and I like the fact that my teenage daughter, who doesn't remember me working in a demanding, professional role all those years ago, has a working mum role model doing something she enjoys.

What advice would I give someone looking to start their own business?

Make sure there's a demand for what you plan to do; I was fortunate enough to have contacts in the industry who could help me understand current demand before I set up shop.

Read the small print – if I had done this with the HCPC stuff, I probably would have started the business considerably earlier.

Be persistent when you come up against challenges – you'll get through them in the end, as I did when trying to find a supervisor.

Don't try to do everything yourself; know what you're good at and where you need help. I'm not a web designer, a brand specialist or an accountant (and lots of other things besides), so I have made use of the SAB network to obtain the services I need – and I'm sure there will be more of this as I go on. It's worth paying for others' expertise not just for peace of mind but also to get things done faster and more skilfully.

Use any free business advice or grants going; I took advantage of the start-up support from STANTA which led to a very useful and thought-provoking strategy session (with a list of action points for me to do) and free workshops on various business topics.

Find a trusted advisor/confidante/mate who you can talk to about your hopes and fears for the business and who can provide a shoulder to cry on/endless cups of tea/glasses of wine as and when needed and will help you retain a sense of perspective.

Don't neglect your own development; I must have continuing professional development as part of my registration but in any event, I'm keen to stay updated and acquire new skills, and see that as an important part of my personal investment in the business.

Set yourself reasonable goals and GO FOR IT!

NICKY WEISFELD
www.valuingminds.com

DANIELLE DURANT
The Cobbled Kitchen

"It's now, or never, Danielle." So said my teaching colleague and dear friend one September day in 2013. We had just been talking about the stresses and strains of secondary school teaching when also trying to run a home and be a mum to two, not always easy, boys.

My last teaching post finished the previous July. It nearly finished me. I had become a serial maternity-cover teacher and had underestimated the toll of working in different schools for just a few months at a time. And the thought of going back after a term's "break" just filled me with dread.

I've always been a creative person, enjoying making things whether it was out of mud and junk as a young child or fabrics, thread or even wood veneer as I got older. And I always knew I'd follow in my dad's footsteps at some point in my life – relying on my own hands to earn a living. But before that, thanks to a particular teacher of mine in the Sixth Form, I discovered the love of learning and teaching. So I took that route from University onwards and thoroughly enjoyed it for many years. Until 2013.

With fewer opportunities to be creative and produce things in adult life, this outlet was found in cooking. I'm a foodie; I love eating and I love feeding people. My mum and I have often felt fundamentally connected with the cultures and peoples (mainly women) around the world, throughout history at that very moment a pot of homemade food is put on the table and the family dives in. Heaven.

So I was faced with the choice – classroom or kitchen? A chance chat after dropping off the kids one morning with another mum, the incredibly clever Sinead, who I had no idea worked for Ogilvy & Mather and later, Saatchi & Saatchi, felt like the stars had aligned themselves right above me in the sky. She told me to jot my ideas down on the back of an envelope for her. The creative juices started flowing again, excitement at the thought of combining all of my passions into a Name that didn't yet exist or a Logo that no-one had yet seen, was simply irresistible. It wouldn't leave me. A late night chat with Andy, my husband (who's great with words and plays on words, although also thinks this is all you need to make a joke!) revealed that Name. After mentioning to him that when we were kids, my brother and I never knew what was for dinner because our mum made it up as she went along and called it "some concoction" – The Cobbled Kitchen was born.

Through Sinead's brand designer friend, I soon got to see the Logo. Well actually, there were several, but she left the best till last and when I first saw MY aubergine coloured pot with exquisite, varied font lettering like random ingredients, I cried. I actually shed tears and I wanted to show my mum immediately, as she knows what a big pot means.

With Andy supporting me, I could then spend most of 2014 supporting my parents. My father became very ill and my mother and I drove everyday for a month to and from the hospital. Once he was back home, I could spend time trying to cobble together my own website. Well, I couldn't afford to pay someone to do it for me. It soon became very apparent that there is an astonishing amount of talent and expertise standing around in school playgrounds at 9 and 3pm every day up and down the country. Mums, dads, carers and grandparents, who are experts in their fields including (usefully) marketing, retail, food buying, research, design, technology, accounting, book-keeping, stuff I'd never heard of yet needed, and if it wasn't there, they'd know which direction to point me in. So from the outset, I have found wonderful people who offered their time and energy towards helping me, when I didn't have a clue what to do. I started using phrases like "responsive websites", "upselling" and "SEO" which had never crossed my lips before.

It was the mums and kids in that very same playground who also became my guinea-pigs and "market research base". I didn't have to find my ideal market theoretically, they were there in front of me – parents, of a certain demographic and socio-economic strata, who needed help with feeding their families in a world that makes the basics of life pressurised and complex. They answered my questionnaires, tasted my food and came along to learn how to cook in my home kitchen. They trusted me with their children in the school holidays to teach them to cook using real knives! It was fun, social, educational, therapeutic me-time, inspiring, creative and productive – for me as well as them!

It was one of those mums who had heard about a meeting in a local pub for new businesses and asked if I'd like to go with her – neither of us felt we could go alone. In the end, there were only 3 or 4 of us in total. My business cards and fliers became my power dressing heels – so I felt I could pretend to be a new business. I remember wondering how long I could use the term "Start-up" for and 3 years later, I still find refuge in that forgiving description. "Mumpreneur" is another. But I found my business home. The group quickly grew, became known as St Albans Businesses or affectionately referred to as SABs and we became SABBERs. The loneliness of working at home without heating (I couldn't justify putting it on for just me) soon evaporated and once again, I was happily part of a community. It was just like the staff room at school, where you could be honest with each other about anything. Now, once a month, we can offload about the bits of running a business we can't do on our own, or even about our family lives, how there's no time for anything etc, etc. This is all the networking I wanted. Real people, real lives – no one minute timed sales pitches, promises to thank, refer or connect. It just happens naturally.

There's a reason why most of this account is about me, the concept and the beginning. I've been told many a time to believe in myself, to believe I'm a businesswoman, and to believe that The Cobbled Kitchen is a real business. I'll always be me first and then a mum. Once a teacher, always a teacher. (That usually means doing stuff just because it's the right thing to do, not because you get paid for it.) I just want to help and inspire people to cook more from scratch at home, creatively and instinctively, eat together as family and community, share their love and time for others through food. If that means my business is a hobby, so be it. But it is all mine.

DANIELLE DURANT
www.thecobbledkitchen.co.uk

SUZY MOODY

Home Start Hertfordshire

Support and friendship for families

So this is me, Suzy Moody. Some would say that I am the face of Home-Start in St Albans, others just say I get around a lot!

I have, what is called in the trade, a 'blended family', which consists of four children (two are step), a Husband and a dog (also step). I say 'children' loosely, as two of them are 20 and the other two are 17 and 15.

In addition, I have also been promoted recently and now proudly wear the title of Grandma to a gorgeous little girl.

I started my career in Bucks County Council, social care team, working with young people in a residential children's home. This was a baptism of fire, best described as character building!

The highlights of my first couple of weeks consisted of being chased across the garden by a police dog - a case of mistaken identity; ducking a dinner that was launched across the room and cooking for 11 teenagers, I took it as a good sign that my dinner was not thrown across the room.

Joking aside, these young people had experienced things in their short lives that no adult should experience in a lifetime. Every child I worked with had a great personality and real character, but sadly their childhood experiences, that had landed them in the care system, had caused huge scars and for some, their behaviour was at times erratic, violent and self-destructive.

My journey continued in Children and Families services, fuelled by the experiences I'd had in the children's home. Over the next six years I worked in several roles in education and health, all focused around supporting families who were in crisis, and children (9+ yrs) who were vulnerable and at risk.

I liked the challenge, no day was ever the same, which sometimes was a blessing, and I liked the fact that what I did could make a difference to some. (Check out The starfish story at the end of this one).

The highs and lows of working with families in crisis can be extreme. Getting a young person back to school or supporting a family to enable them to get their children back home are great moments; but conversely, seeing generational cycles of destructive behaviour resulting in children being removed, or working with a family where a young person has attempted suicide, are the really tough days.

I had by now worked out two things; firstly, that it was harder to effect change with older children as patterns of behaviour were so ingrained and secondly, that whatever support the child receives, it is ineffective if the environment they live in remains the same.

Part of this realisation was also probably down to the fact that I now had two children and had faced some challenges of my own in the last couple of years.

So my focus changed to early intervention parenting support and I re-trained in this area. A short time later, the government put parenting at the top of their agenda and released a huge amount of funding to develop parenting services.

This opened up a great and much needed opportunity to develop parenting support across the County that was accessible to all and could truly deliver early intervention and preventative support.

My vision became a reality and I set up and ran a countywide parenting support service, which was fantastic. Training was available, delivery was consistent across the County and we had removed the stigma of parenting support being for parents that are failing.

Three years later due to a few life changing events, I moved to St Albans to be with my now husband. I took a bit of time out of work to look after me and to be there for my children.

Then came Home-Start!

It seemed the perfect job, Manager of St Albans scheme (as it was then), a bit of management, direct family support and all about children and families. Note that I don't mention fundraising and event management as at that point it was just a small feature of the job.

I joined a team of two, Donna and Claire, (three staff had recently left). They were brilliant, friendly and positive, open to making changes and developing the scheme. Part of the development was to build links with local businesses, so with trepidation, I stepped into the corporate world, having been very institutionalised after 18 years in County Council, this was a real eye opener – expenses account, what's that?!

Home-Start is not a crisis intervention service and is not statutory, so we work with families before they go into crisis and are able to engage with harder to reach families as we don't have the stigma of being a local authority service.

Eighteen months in, my role changed as our County funding was withdrawn and we needed to raise £40,000 to continue.

I reduced my case load and concentrated on fundraising, something that I had no previous experience of. I learned lots about crowd funding, event organisation and I also learned that when a reporter calls you and asks some questions, your answers are printed verbatim.

We raised £38,000, enough to keep us going until Christmas, and by then we were at the point of agreeing a merge with six other schemes across the County.

So here I am now, Strategic Manager of Home-Start Herts – a role which is about PR, communications, income generation, building corporate partnerships, event management; not a role I would have ever envisaged myself in, but I love it.

There is no direct family work in the role but I am fine with that, my passion for the work is fuelled by the amazing people I meet and work alongside and the unbelievable support that we receive from the community and business'.

Star Fish Story

Once upon a time, there was an old man who used to go to the ocean to do his writing. He had a habit of walking on the beach every morning before he began his work. Early one morning, he was walking along the shore after a big storm had passed and found the vast beach littered with starfish as far as the eye could see, stretching in both directions.

Off in the distance, the old man noticed a small boy approaching. As the boy walked, he paused every so often and as he grew closer, the man could see that he was occasionally bending down to pick up an object and throw it into the sea. The boy came closer still and the man called out, "Good morning! May I ask what it is that you are doing?"

The young boy paused, looked up, and replied "Throwing starfish into the ocean. The tide has washed them up onto the beach and they can't return to the sea by themselves," the youth replied.

"When the sun gets high, they will die, unless I throw them back into the water."

The old man replied, "But there must be tens of thousands of starfish on this beach. I'm afraid you won't really be able to make much of a difference."

The boy bent down, picked up yet another starfish and threw it as far as he could into the ocean.

Then he turned, smiled and said,
"It made a difference to that one!"

SUZY MOODY
www.home-startherts.org.uk

DEBORAH TEMPLE

DST*design*

Interior Designer, DST Design

Drowning in deadlines, bureaucracy and feeling like a number and undervalued... I am sure this will resound with many... and this is why I started my business journey.

It was a "reaching the cross roads" moment (enough was enough). I had been working for the same company for 10 years. I was good at my job, and my managers knew it, and so at first you don't notice the increase in work until it is too late! I was over-worked, stressed and often in tears - the first signs of depression!

Luckily I'm stubborn and highly motivated. I can't say it was easy, but with the support of my then boyfriend (now wonderful husband) I handed in my notice.

It was the best thing I ever did. It was the first stepping stone...

Find your passion... If you do something you are passionate about this shines through and people gravitate towards you. Creativity was my passion and I was hungry to seek it out. I had no idea at the time I would become an Interior Designer (it wasn't on the radar). My journey was long (14 years) as it was interspersed with becoming the perpetual student, working, getting married, and raising a family. Life is a juggling act...

In brief, I spent 4 years at University studying a business degree. Great! It was a fun time and I learnt the skills to set up and run my own company. Um what company? What did I want to do?

Back to work... finance... HUH, "not very creative!" I hear you say, but being a student doesn't pay the bills!

More studying, whilst working full-time. I attended evening courses in jewellery smithing, garden design and then Interior Design. Wow, Loved it, it ticked all the boxes. Next to qualify as an Interior Designer, so yes you guessed it another 8 years of study, and working part-time, being a mum full-time, until somewhat nervously I created DST Design Ltd.

Nervous was an understatement, but could I do it! YES! With my stubbornness to succeed and much thanks to a very patient husband (who has high hopes of early retirement!), and business acquaintances along the way.

The biggest challenge is getting your name out there. It took a good year before people appreciated the extent of how I could help. It was a learning curve on how to market yourself and inspire people. Interior Design is featured on TV and certainly in the 80's and early 90's it didn't get the best of reputations. I had to convince people that Interior Design is actually for the normal person with a normal budget and normal problems such as challenging room layouts. And I was definitely not a "cushion fluffer".

My strength is space planning and full house renovations, with a passion for ensuring the interior space is in tune with the person's lifestyle.

Networking was (and still remains) a necessary part of my working week. It can help you start-up and grow your business. I still remember the first time I went networking, yet again another daunting task, but it's one of the best things you can do for you and your business. I remember I was so shy and retiring... not any more. You learn, build confidence and receive such great support from other businesses. It's like a comfort blanket.

Running your own business has its trials and tribulations, but you don't have to do it alone! Surround yourself with good positive people who do also become your pool of resources. I have found that although I am a control freak, you can't be a jack of all trades and do it all yourself. It's just not good business sense. For a business to succeed I've learnt to concentrate on the core profit making parts of the business (design consultation) which is what I'm passionate about. It is after all, why I started this journey. Seek advice, and find people who can help you streamline your processes so you spend less time on unavoidable and mundane admin, accounting or marketing processes. I've learnt to be an advocate of outsourcing and not being afraid to ask for help. It applies in particular to the forever changing world of marketing and social media. I'm always looking for tips on the best and new ways to attract the ideal client. Networking isn't just about business... I am so privileged to have forged some great friendships and business partnerships along the way and these have all helped to grow my business and my confidence.

I am lucky that I have found my work passion in life. We spend so many hours working, so we should at least enjoy it. The perfect work life balance doesn't exist as life is full of curve balls to shake things up. On occasions, in busy periods, I may be working very long hours, but the difference is that I'm doing it because I choose too. I exist being "ME" and was never ever going to be the stay at home housewife or mum. I am proud to be the master of my own diary so I'm always there for my family!

I often like to retort that "Starting up a business is a bit like having a baby. If you waited for the right time then it would probably never happen". As your business matures over the years there are different challenges to face. You need to nurture your customers, contractors and business partners, (and of course yourself) and yes they will throw their toys out of their pram (like I do occasionally), but who said that running a business is easy.

My company has grown from strength to strength and I am happier in control of my own life, doing something I very much enjoy and am passionate about.

So is it worth the hard graft? Oh definitely without a doubt!

DEBORAH TEMPLE
www.dstdesign.co.uk

AMANDA DILWORTH
Ruby and Freddies

Let me introduce you to Ruby and Freddie, my grandparents, and the inspiration behind the brand. It may have all begun with a nappy cake for my best friend's baby shower but the drive and determination most certainly comes from Ruby and Freddie.

Freddie was a self-made businessman who dedicated his life to creating and building his own business. Ruby had a passion for retail, working in family owned cafes in London and opening a wool shop in Hove. In addition, my mother and brother both run their own businesses and therefore I thought it was about time I should do the same.

So in 2012, with the support of my family, hubby Nick and daughters Grace and Daisy, the concept of Ruby and Freddies became a reality and I opened the proverbial doors.

We started from humble beginnings: my original aim was to make nappy cakes for friends and relatives for baby showers. Before your stomachs begin rumbling, nappy cakes aren't actually cakes – they contain various baby products including nappies and baby clothing made to look like a cake! Once I had made a few sales, I started to look at how I could improve my product suppliers as I was purchasing direct from high street stores which was expensive and whose manufacturing methods and origins were out of my control.

I wanted to make sure the products in the nappy cakes were high quality and unique and the only way I could achieve this aim was to oversee the design and manufacture the products myself. At the centre of this was my desire to manufacture and sell products made in the UK.

We scoured the country for manufacturers that were able to help us with this brief - it wasn't easy, but eventually we found manufacturers in Mansfield, Gloucester and Wembley.

In 2013, Little Londoners (baby grows) and Little Woolies (sweaters) were born. This was a real challenge because I had to put a £10,000 payment down for the manufacturing process which there was no guarantee I would get back. In addition, working with manufacturers who would often prioritise bigger customers was very difficult. We had mixed success and this taught me how important distribution and marketing can be. At this stage, we were only able to distribute through our own website and a limited number of wholesalers and I couldn't afford any additional online advertising. Social media and promotion had to come directly from me, so I taught myself how to use Twitter, Instagram and Facebook. Despite the high quality product and design, sales for Little Woolies were poor. This phase of the business and a kind Selfridges buyer taught me to be ruthless - if an idea isn't working, you need to stop, re-assess, and change. This may be by selling off the stock to recoup costs or by re-targeting accordingly.

Thankfully, our good ongoing wholesale relationships and good sales from Little Londoners made enough money to continue the business and focus on launching some new concepts.

Our next breakthrough came in 2014, when we were accepted as a Partner on NotontheHighStreet.com, rapidly increasing our sales, driving traffic directly to our website and giving us greater credibility with wholesalers. After two years of hard graft for not much reward, this now felt more like a business than a hobby. It was at this stage that I realised how important it was to be organised: when you are dealing with between 30-40 orders per day during peak times, as well as juggling wholesale orders and looking after two kids, a dog and a husband, it can be tricky! Thankfully, my Dad, has saved the day several times during my busy phases, stepping in to help me pack up and send out orders.

Selling through the 'Not on the High Street' platform made me realise that products don't need to be complicated. They need to be high quality and unique to make a real difference in that market place. This is when I started to streamline my range and came up with the idea of the baby bouquet which is now my best seller. The last couple of years have seen my sales more than triple, this has meant that I am able to pay myself a salary and look towards a future full of possibilities for the business.

Last year, I felt confident enough to approach some of the big retail brands in London. I sent numerous emails, made various phone calls, sent several LinkedIn requests and drew on the networks of fellow SABers (St Albans Businesses) and local business contacts to put me in touch with contacts at these brands. After many months of hard slog it was at this stage that I thought I had achieved success – a very prestigious London hotel based in Mayfair wanted to stock my products. We agreed on terms and I got the manufacturing process underway. However, a month later, my contact at the hotel left and the partnership was cancelled! I was distraught, how could they do this?! In some respects, it was good timing – it was the run up to Christmas and I was able to put all my efforts into improving my platform and website sales. I was determined that when I next approached the big brand retail names it would be with a knock-out product that they couldn't refuse!

This year has seen continued improvements in my revenues, despite challenging business conditions. I am excited about the future: we have just released our boxed baby bouquets which are a breakthrough product and I hope can take our business to the next level. I believe that I have the knock-out product I mentioned to take to the luxury retail outlets and I am confident that my product would sit comfortably along other luxury items brands around the world.

I have achieved a lot in my five and a half years since beginning Ruby and Freddies. Most of all running my own business has taught me stubbornness, resilience but, most of all, to enjoy the journey because you never know what is around the corner! I couldn't have done it without the support of family, friends, and wonderful business networks such as SABs and the NOTHS Partner Support network.

AMANDA DILWORTH
www.rubyandfreddies.co.uk

ADARSH MEHTA

Let's Talk Travel – Road to Entrepreneurship

Well, I had been working in the pharmaceutical industry for the best part of 12 years. I was pretty comfortable with my position despite the long shifts involved – sometimes I would work 6 to 7 days a week. At the back of my mind, there had always been a part of me wanting to change, a different life. However, I never summoned the courage to take that first step.

The major deal breaker for me came when I was told that the pharmaceutical business would be sold. I knew at this point that the time was now or never. Besides, I had to decide between applying for jobs or starting a new business venture. I would say it was as a result of a reaction to the circumstance at that time rather than an action. I am glad things have turned out the way they have and I still believe everything happens for a reason.

My venture into the travel business took me months of planning and study – which began even before I left my job at the pharmaceutical company. I liked what I found after my research and was convinced the business was viable – with effort, I could make it a success. People are still travelling. Whether it is within the country or abroad, people are still going on holidays, destination weddings, honeymoons and sporting trips. People are also still seeking adventures in places that they have little knowledge about. This is where us agents can help and give the expert advice to make clients' travels as smooth as possible.

Every industry has its challenges and the travel industry is no different. Despite the fact the travel industry is one of the largest industries, there was always a fear it was dominated by the existing established companies. As a rookie trying to break into the travel business, I was frightened by the competition. So, I think the biggest challenge we faced was having to compete with these more established businesses. We also had many other notable storms we had to tame to arrive at this point.

I would say our biggest achievement was being able to take a moment and realize after 2 years of intense struggle that we were where we wanted to be. Of course, the recognitions have been coming in terms of awards and accolades. Don't get me wrong, it feels good to be recognized by your peers in the industry. But the major sense of fulfilment for me is seeing clients tell us that we have been able to take most of the burden off – by what we do, showing appreciation for what we are doing and spurring us to do better.

Nothing beats the thought of you being in control of your life – I like being in control! Having to earn a living doing what I love to do and how I want to do it. I don't think there is anything more satisfying than that. And knowing that the future of my family depends on decisions that I make.

I find the work very refreshing and satisfying. Even though I enjoyed my previous job with the pharmaceutical company, the travel business isn't a job in my opinion – I find it a passion and a hobby. And having to earn a living out of my hobby is simply a blessing. Most importantly, running my own business gives me so much time to spend doing other things I love – like spend more quality time with my family, catch up with friends and do sports on a more regular basis.

I think life as an entrepreneur changed a lot of things for me. Most notable of them all is that I have a new found passion for work. I have to think about things critically before making even the slightest decision – like the need to make an early morning phone call before having a cup of tea! As a consequence of my type of work, I deal with a lot of people every day; I find myself always learning new things and different approaches to situations I would never have imagined before.

From the very first day I opened for business, the motivation has come naturally to me. I believe every human is naturally allergic to failure. So to an extent, I would say the fear of failure keeps me going every day.

I'm inspired by the people I meet and the joy they bring me when they narrate how they find peace and happiness in what they do. People who never give up no matter what and see the positives in every situation. People who will go the extra mile to lend a helping hand or good advice during times of need. People who come together to create strength in numbers to contribute to something that creates change. People are my inspiration!

The saying "Fail to prepare, Prepare to fail" is sufficient enough. Any admission I could possibly give would do no more justice. In fact, those words of wisdom should be hanging on the ceiling of your bedroom so that they are the last thing you see before going to bed and the first thing when you wake up.

You must plan the business. You must plan on the business, and you must plan for the future of the business.

ADARSH MEHTA
www.letstalktravel.co.uk

NICKY PACKMAN

FOREVER **Forever Living**

It seems rather fitting that I am writing this as I enter the last week of my Forties.

Time to reflect on what has been a rollercoaster of a decade that has seen me raise two children with my wonderful partner, become my own boss and gradually grow an income stream from across the globe. Here's my story ...

I never knew what I wanted to do when I grew up. As a child, I spent several years living on a farm in Cornwall and often helped - well, I like to think so anyway - the farmer get the cows in from the field of an evening. Maybe I would work with animals. Horses, maybe – that was every girl's dream, right? But then we moved back to London and I was distracted by boys. No, not in that way. They played football and I discovered I loved spending hours and hours kicking a ball around with them in the park. Jumpers for goalposts. Yes, that's it, I'll be a professional footballer! Alas, back then there were no such opportunities on the horizon for budding female players. Something would come up I'm sure.

After a rather mediocre time at school which I mostly hated - thank goodness for Duran Duran and Smash Hits magazine to keep me smiling through those years - I spent four successful years at college studying Business. That gave me a good grounding in many aspects of the working world, but I still wasn't clear what to do next. Thankfully, I then had a lucky break – a friend was working at a company in London and they needed a Secretary. And so my 17 year career in the Magazine

Publishing Industry commenced and I was given more responsibility over the years taking on the roles of Office Manager and Senior HR Assistant.

At the ripe old age of 37 (and a half!) I had my first child, and whilst on maternity leave I realised that I had absolutely no desire to return to the daily commute and stresses of corporate life. Besides, childcare was going to cost me an absolute fortune and I couldn't imagine leaving my son with anyone else. So I quit.

For the next few years motherhood was all-consuming – my daughter was born and life was good. However, in 2009 I felt I wanted to find a way to bring some extra income into the household – and to get stuck into something to stimulate my squidgy mummy brain. Options were limited – I didn't want to put my kids into childcare and I wanted to be able to work flexibly from home. Good fortune came my way when a friend mentioned she was working alongside a global company in the health and wellbeing marketplace. I borrowed some products from her for a few days to see why she was so excited. I could see how the products may be able to benefit my family and friends, but I was very sceptical about the business model as it all seemed far to be good to be true. However, after my own extensive research, I decided I had nothing to lose by giving it a go. What's the worst that could happen?

I bought some products and started my journey with Forever Living Products. I became a sponge – I read everything I possibly could about the products and business, attended all the trainings and became a product of my products. After all, how could I ethically recommend them to others if I didn't have belief in them myself?

My first challenge was that I am not a sales person – I dislike the feeling of being sold to and I didn't want to be someone that people avoided. I had to learn how best to share the benefits of the products and realised that letting people try things for a few days before deciding whether to buy was the way to go. That was comfortable and my customer base grew, as did the number of repeat orders.

The second challenge was that many people were dismissive of my attempt to build a team of independent distributors – they were as sceptical as I had been about the network marketing business model when I first looked at it. I found this hard, as people were not always particularly pleasant in the way that they conveyed their thoughts. And it hurt. I have had to learn not to take their rejection to heart.

Social Media has been a help and hindrance in equal measure in my opinion – sadly there will always be those keyboard warrior 'trolls' ready to give their views, often driven by misinformation and lack of a true understanding of exactly how network marketing works when done in the RIGHT way.

Fast forward 8 years and through hard work and dedication my business has continued to expand steadily - I have a healthy, growing income stream from the UK and several other countries around the world. Helping people with both the products and the business opportunity has been exciting. Watching team members grow in confidence as they expand their own businesses is particularly rewarding. I have learned a lot of business skills since I started, but I had not anticipated the personal development that has underpinned my journey so far - I am doing things now that I would never in a million years have thought I would attempt, stepping outside of my comfort zone in so many ways. I have grown as a person and feel far more empowered than ever before.

For anyone considering starting their own business, my advice would be to do your research, check your sums and, if it all adds up, take a leap of faith. It's such an exciting and rewarding journey in so many ways. Inevitably there will be challenges, so make sure you have a strong 'Why' that will motivate you to keep going should things get tough. Don't let anyone steal your dream. Here's to an exciting future!

NICKY PACKMAN
www.nickypackman.com

GILL TURTON

lifeadmin lifeadmin

The concept of lifeadmin goes way beyond being a business. Our mission is to free people's time, inspiring them to enjoy life. lifeadmin promotes wellbeing, health and happiness by liberating people from their growing to-do list so they can spend time doing what they love.

Having spent over 10 years working in corporate business as a Personal Assistant I felt it was time to take control of my own life. I had noticed a shift in culture at the work place and it was having a direct impact not only on my life, but my colleagues' and friends' as well. The working day is rarely 9-5 anymore, and it struck me that both businesses and individuals need to adapt better to this new way of working in order to maintain a healthy, profitable and happy work-life balance.

Friends and family would always label me as the 'organiser' for any event or trip and the 'problem solver' for any tech fault or finding a birthday present. Soon, friends of friends were contacting me and asking me to solve these lifestyle tasks for them. I started to think about how I could combine these skills with the trust people put in me as a 'solver' and make it my day job.

So, that's when I created lifeadmin.

Working with a range of clients, from business owners and start-ups to parents and young professionals, means every day is different. Engaging with such a variety of people to solve their challenges keeps me motivated and there is no better feeling when our service helps others and makes a difference in their lives. Being part of a community enables me to meet so many inspiring people, who dedicate their time to helping others, be that in business or life. In turn, that inspires me to focus on the core of lifeadmin's mantra: to free your time.

Of course, it hasn't been plain sailing. Taking the plunge into self-employment and starting your own business brings with them inherent risks. For me, it was a step into the unknown, into a new community and the start of an entirely new life. But I had done my research, and, most importantly, had unwavering belief in the unique service that I offered and the mission I was on.

It's been particularly challenging to maintain a long-term vision and focus on developing lasting relationships, when it is natural to want short-term gains to satisfy your financial demands of running a business. I have had to be agile too, ensuring that the long-term strategy remains in view but allowing different routes to get there.

Strategy and planning are so important for any business, but especially a new one. A plan helps to remind you of your objectives, which is important when you have inevitable doubts. It's also important to celebrate your achievements, big or small. It's not easy to take a step back from everything when you're in the thick of it, managing clients, networking and getting your head around digital marketing, but measuring your success and celebrating it are vital. I gave myself a big pat on the pack for setting everything up, including the website, something which I had never done before. I get a great sense of achievement when

I walk into people's homes or offices, the way relief washes over their faces makes me so glad I started lifeadmin. Through hard work and dedication, my business has gone from a bright idea to a brand supporting local people, businesses, events and even the local football club. Not only am I very proud but I'm also really excited for what the future will bring. That's a feeling I never had working full-time for someone else.

Doing something that I love and am passionate about has always been important to me, so when I go to work now, it doesn't feel like a chore or something I'd rather not do. Everyone is so busy these days, it's increasingly hard to find that sought-after work-life balance. But I was determined to find the best formula, and now I've found it, I want to help others do the same. I am on a mission to give people their time back, so they can spend it doing something they love and make their own amazing stories.

GILL TURTON
www.lifeadmin.uk.com

LOUISE BRENNAN
Louise's Antenatal Classes

Hi, my name is Louise Brennan. I am a qualified nurse and midwife working in the NHS since 2001.

I set up my first business in 2006, with a brilliant midwife friend. We had been concerned for some time about the level of information that women seemed to have when they were admitted in labour. There were often negative misconceptions and/or a lack of knowledge surrounding things like epidurals or cesarean sections.

After spending time talking to our colleagues and to women, we discovered that often the information taught in antenatal classes seemed to be contributing to this lack of knowledge.

From this, we developed our plans for teaching private antenatal classes that discussed the realities of having a baby but that also built confidence in both the women's ability to birth her baby and how her birth partner could help and support her.

After months of planning, our business 'BirthingMatters' was born! We had our first class in July 2006 and two couples attended!

We went from strength to strength and had seven amazing and successful years. Sadly in 2013, for personal reasons, I left the business. This greatly upset me at the time as I loved what we did and what we had achieved.

In 2014, I wanted to start up another business and wanted it to involve antenatal classes. The most popular classes that I taught in Hertfordshire while with BirthingMatters were one to one classes. As this was my local area, it gave me the idea to start a business solely offering private one to one classes. The advantage of this is the classes are tailored around the couple rather than them having to fit into group class times and dates. It also means that we can discuss any topic they wish rather than a set group class programme.

Louise's Antenatal Classes was born in December 2014!

I didn't do much with the business throughout the early part of 2015 due moving house and other personal issues but started devoting some energy to it around mid-June. It took six months to get a website up and running so by the start of 2016, I was raring to go!

My aim for 2016 was to have one class a month. From June to November 2016, I ran around 1-3 classes per month. I was delighted with this as it had exceeded my expectations. I was loving what I was doing, mostly still NHS work but my own business on the side.

In 2017, I started offering birth reflection sessions. These sessions are for any women or couples who are upset or feel traumatised by their birth experience and wish to talk about it. It's an opportunity to try to understand what and why things happened the way they did. It also involves planning for the next pregnancy, if appropriate. This is open to women of all ages, it doesn't matter how long ago the birth was, and I would happily meet anyone who wants to talk about their birth experience.

The most satisfying part about running my classes is seeing couples who may be frightened or nervous about birth before the class, and then afterwards feeling more positive and confident about the process. I love hearing from the couples I meet and hearing about how their birth went. I really enjoy helping people and imparting my knowledge. I have women stay in touch with me for months after their baby has been born and this is just wonderful. I get pictures and updates as to how their babies are doing.

At the moment, I have the best of both worlds. I still have my NHS work which I love and will never stop.

Being with women and their families is ultimately my role as a midwife but I also get to teach classes which I enjoy so much. I feel very lucky and don't want this dual working to end!

However, starting a business in a social media driven era has been an eye opener and my biggest struggle! Prior to this, I used Facebook but I taught myself how to use Twitter in the start of 2016.

Advertising this business and getting my voice out there is still the biggest struggle that I face! I have joined Pinterest but haven't a clue what I am doing on there! It all feels very different to when we set up BirthingMatters. I spend quite a lot of my evenings on social media. I have joined networking groups such as St Albans Businesses. I haven't managed to attend the main networking 'jelly' group but I hope to in the future. I have attended some of the social meetings though. It's great to network with other business people and form working partnerships. The other struggle I have is keeping up with the books but once I get into completing them, I quite enjoy it!

There are a couple of things that motivate and inspire me in my business. The first is receiving that first email enquiry from a couple. I find the initial contact is always really exciting with the prospect of meeting another lovely couple. The other is just after I have finished teaching a class. Once I know the couple have understood everything and are feeling more confident, I get a feeling of elation that I have helped another couple. I then start looking forward to hearing from them after they have had their baby and finding out how the birth went.

Running my own business has given me more freedom in my working life. It means I can do more of what I enjoy and brings a good balance of my classes and clinical work. I would recommend to anyone to start their own business. My advice would be to research your product/service first. Find some local networking groups, they are invaluable to meet other business owners. My last piece of advice is to keep going! It is hard work running your own business. It can be lonely at times and you will have ups and downs; busy and quiet periods and you need to find a way to keep yourself motivated. I find that remembering why I do what I do is great motivation. Good luck!

LOUISE BRENNAN
www.louantenatal.com/

JAMES SHEEHAN
Macpro Design and Print Ltd.

I was in my early 40's when I decided it was the right time to set up my own business. As lovely as it would be to say that Macpro Design and Print was born out of some grand vision, I am afraid the truth was far simpler than that. I had been on the tail end of redundancies a few times and the firm I was working for started to go in a different direction, experience told me that it would not work (sadly it didn't).

Having worked successfully within the print and design industry since the age of 16, I was confident I had the right blend of skills, knowledge and expertise to run my own business. With the children in higher education and my wife working, it made the financial implications feel less of a risk than if I had tried this earlier on in life. With that in mind I took the decision to start up on my own and have no regrets.

I began as a sole trader and provided design, artwork and reprographic services (whereby files are prepared to plate for Litho printing) for local printers in Hertfordshire. The network of contacts I had gained already throughout my career proved invaluable to me. They provided me with work, new contacts / clients as well as offering help and advice for which I am very grateful and am still in touch with many of them today.

Fast forward twenty years and the business has evolved. Macpro Design & Print moved from sole trader status to a limited company. The rest of my family have joined me in the business and we are currently a team of four with my wife, son and daughter all key players in its operation. We provide a full range of artwork, design and print solutions for our clients but due to changes in the industry the reprographic side of the business is minimal. The decline of the reprographic work was a notable challenge in Macpro Design & Print's history and led to a change in direction for the business. The rise of the internet and the digital era caused a decline in print, in particular a significant reduction in offset printing for high volume runs. Rather than dwell on this we embraced it. We invested in more machinery / equipment and moved into digital printing in 2006.

Our values remained the same but our focus changed as client orders became smaller and often more demanding. This side of the business has continued to expand and develop to also include post-printing enhancements; adding additional value to printed material and helping clients strengthen their brand.

Moving into the digital printing arena has been a great learning curve and wasn't always easy to start with but we did our best, applied our experience and are proud of what the business has become. It taught us the importance of not being complacent. It's crucial to have a clear path of what you are working towards but also to stay fluid and adapt when required. By following these principles our business has been able to move forward and grow.

For me, I have found that personal fulfilment is the most satisfying thing about running my own business. It's completely different to being employed as you create your own future and there is a real sense of achievement. Being your own boss constantly pushes you out of your comfort zone but in doing so you realise you must rise to these challenges. It keeps you on your toes. You are continually learning and looking for new opportunities. I have developed a number of skills and values that only running a business will ever teach you.

Life has completely changed since starting up and I'm not sure anything could have prepared me for this, at times it has seemed like a second marriage. It's not all about the money – in fact there are some days when we all feel we would earn more working for someone else but that quickly passes and none of us would ever want to or could go back to "9 – 5 roles".

The business is part of me and now part of our family, we enjoy working together.

So why do we do it? We know what a difference good print can make and there is strong scientific evidence that supports this. This is what drives our business. We want print to thrive and benefit many businesses. We love how print is tactile, engaging and can add credibility. It is our aim to utilise this and always provide excellent work at competitive prices.

It's our clients that keep us motivated and positive feedback always gives us a huge boost. We want to achieve the best for them and often find our own boundaries are stretched and our business develops because of this. One of my proudest achievements is the fact that we have kept a major client retained for two decades. It has been fantastic to see their brand go from strength to strength.

Working with so many great clients and getting to know them along the way we are always inspired by their stories both personally and in business.

What I would say to anyone who is thinking of starting their own business - be prepared to work harder than you ever have in any of your previous employments. You need to be everything from cleaner to boss and wear many hats. You must stay positive; to quote Diane von Furstenberg "Attitude is everything". There are always struggles; every day, week and month which you will need to face head on and overcome but that's the life of a business owner. The rewards for running your own business are unparalleled.

(Left to right: Gail Carman, Deb Sheehan, James Sheehan, Lee Sheehan)

If you know you have the skills and drive then why not go for it rather than building someone else's company?

If you don't give it a try you will never know.

JAMES SHEEHAN
www.macprodp.com

CHRISTINE FRITH

Hour Hands

How did it all happen? I'd love to say that I always had a master plan to set up my own concierge business, but in reality it was more of an organic process. When the youngest Frith started school, I started to get comments along the lines of: "Brilliant, you'll have all the time in the world to clean your house, keep things tidy, how wonderful!" If you know me, you'll understand how much I love my cleaning lady; this was not at all wonderful. I needed to find some work so I could justify keeping her. And so I started to think about what I could do that would fit around family life, and that I would also enjoy.

Having three small boys ridiculously close in age, an old house under renovation (read 'building site') and a husband who worked long hours and travelled a lot, I realised that there were many times when I would have done anything for someone to just come and do jobs for me. Nothing major but things like making necessary phone calls without toddlers screaming in the background, running errands, making bookings – the day-to-day stuff that just takes decades to do with small kids in tow. Keeping three boys alive and our valuables intact was a full-time job, and having someone to deal with my to-do list the size of the kitchen table would have been a dream. One that didn't come true. So I drank coffee and gin, and aged a lot.

In between the coffee and the gin – admittedly a rather narrow window – I realised that I wanted to build a business that could help other busy people. This seemed like a great idea (after the gin) but rather scary (after the coffee), so I went looking for a friend to do it with me. Liz had often talked about leaving her secure London-based job in the public sector, so I used my best persuasive techniques (a series of John Lewis lunches) to convince her that a no-security start-up would be the ideal next step. And Hour Hands was born.

Two and a half years later, we're still here and thriving. Hour Hands has an expanding client list and offers a wide range of services for both business and home. There are now four of us in the company and we're recruiting for even more hands. I'll be honest, it's taken an extreme amount of hard work and no small amount of luck, but we've never looked back.

This is why I think we managed it:

Make a proper business plan

Think carefully about the income you want, or need, to earn from your business. Does it need to cover the mortgage, see the kids through uni, or just fund your shoe habit? After presenting my 'escape from cleaning' idea to my husband, one of his first questions was: "What's it going to cost?" Closely followed by: "And how are you going to make money? Where are your clients coming from?" Not quite the "wonderful idea darling, here's a few thousand pounds to get you going" that I had hoped for, but admittedly valid questions that required proper consideration. I decided early on that my business should require minimal set-up costs and that I was to run no risks – decisions that have helped us to achieve sensible and sustainable growth since day one.

Get advice from friends and contacts

We're very fortunate to live in such an entrepreneurial area; I have some amazing friends who are successful local businesswomen. I knocked on their doors for feedback on my business idea and came out with my first two clients; I'm proud to say they have been with Hour Hands ever since.

Understand what your customer wants

Initially, we struggled to work out exactly what services we should offer. We tried a few ideas that ended up being more trouble than they were worth, so since then we've always talked to our customers as much as possible to work out what they need and want from a business like ours.

Know your pipelines and traffic lights!

I find the most challenging part for a small business is balancing the marketing with doing the actual work. I've read the business books and I know the theory, but in practice it's really tough. Client work always comes first and in busy times it's easy to lose sight of where the next job is coming from. We hit a dry patch a little while ago after a really hectic period, so I took some time to tidy up the website and implement a free CRM system. It has really focused our minds. Now, one look and we know instantly what our pipeline is looking like.

Mistakes are a fact of life – learn from them

We try our best to make people's lives easier, to take away the stress, to magic things off their to-do list, but sometimes we don't meet expectations. It hasn't happened often but I find that one of the hardest things to deal with. But learning from mistakes while always being honest and upfront, however hard that is, works best in these relationships built on trust.

Network constantly and embrace competition

Having worked in big corporations before starting a family, I knew all about internal politics. But networking to make contact with other small businesses was a new experience. I've still got a lot to learn. And standing up in front of a big group to explain who I am and what I do still makes me want to dig a hole and hide. But the friendly SAB (St Albans Businesses) group has been an amazing help; I've met some lovely people and gained some invaluable contacts. Finding a small business community so supportive to each other has been such a welcome surprise. Who knew that competition could be so positive – I've even got work from people doing similar things to me. I've definitely learned to embrace competition rather than to avoid it.

Just go for it!

I never thought I'd be the kind of person who could set up a company, but the 'start small, dream big' philosophy seems to be working for us, so far. There's still a long way to go, but it's been an amazing journey and I've never regretted any of it. I love that every day is different. The feeling of satisfaction when a client with a to-do list the size of their kitchen table tells me we've made their life so much easier. And the thrill of bagging a new client!

One of the things Liz and I have promised each other is that we stop when we're not having fun. And we have a lot of fun. So there's no stopping us now.

CHRISTINE FRITH
www.hourhands.co.uk

JULIE BRIAN
Edie & Rona

Let me begin by telling you that my name is Julie, and I am a stationery addict. My online business is called Edie & Rona and my mission is to get you stylishly organised with amazing stationery, accessories and home décor. This is my story so far.

During my 20 year career in the corporate world, I felt privileged to work with amazing leaders, talented colleagues and some of the world's most recognised brands – Coca Cola, The National Lottery and T-Mobile to name but a few. I learned a tremendous amount about business and more importantly, a lot about myself.

The most important thing I learned is that to feel fulfilled in my work life, I must absolutely LOVE what I do. As many of us do, I sacrificed a lot to my career over the years and when I finally stopped having fun, I realised that I was doing the wrong job. It was time for a change.

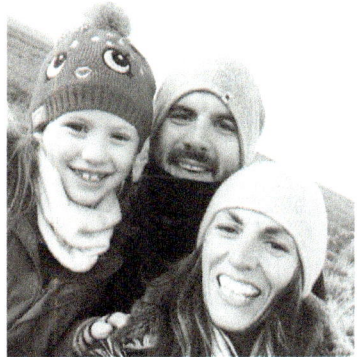

After a life changing trip to Miami, with my husband Chris in 2016, I made a brave decision to leave the security of a 'Times Top 20 Big Company' to set up my own business.

One of the reasons the trip was so important to me was because we stumbled across the most amazing little shop just off the Lincoln Mall called 'Sparkle & Shine, Darling'. Walking through the doors was like walking into elements of the business I had imagined for the past 4 years. It gave me the confidence I needed - if someone else could do it, so could I! Little did I know that the owner of this boutique is a fabulous lady called Adrienne Bosh who is married to Chris Bosh.... An NFL football player in the US! It got me thinking that maybe they have a little more cash in the bank than us?

Regardless, I set the wheels in motion and what a journey it has been. I surprise myself daily at just how much I can achieve in 24 hours. Corporate businesses measure success on the presentation content at each quarterly business review and the progress they can report to the City; it's often slow going when there are so many moving parts.

By comparison, in one calendar quarter, I set up a limited company, designed a brand, produced the logo (with my amazingly talented graphic designer, Zoe McKenzie), built relationships with suppliers from scratch, conducted market research via Pop Ups, launched my Social Media, ran a Christmas campaign and launched a website. My head is still spinning!

I had been collecting ideas for Edie & Rona for almost 3 years before I took the leap to start the company; the concept stemmed from my inability to find inspirational notebooks and stylish desk accessories above & beyond those I could get on the High Street. Throughout my entire career I have worked from home, so my daily motivation had to come from my surroundings, not from my colleagues in an office. I have built a range of products to reflect this, from mixing well known brands with smaller independent companies where I have met some incredibly talented people.

Despite the fun along the way, this has also been the hardest thing I have ever done in my life. Working alone and having fewer people around to bounce ideas off has been a challenge but I have been amazed at the local talent literally on my doorstep here in St. Albans.

It has been a pleasant surprise to realise just how many like-minded people there are working from home building their own empires. They remind me I'm not alone and I have to keep going.

Asked whether I would take the same path again, I would reply 'absolutely'! I feel so lucky that I had an idea that was worth exploring and building into the business I am fortunate to own today. Many ex-colleagues from the corporate world looked on enviously as I left to start this journey because they haven't had their idea yet. Hang in there because you will, if it's something you really believe it.

Finally, many people ask about the name of the company – who are Edie & Rona? Well, they were two incredible Ladies who have been extremely important to my family. Rona was my Nanna and Edie was my husband's Grandma.

Our Grandmothers never met but were from a time of handwritten notes, love letters and endless to do lists. They didn't have online calendars to sync families, email reminders flashing up on multiple screens or an all-knowing search engine to help them.

Instead, they were organised & lived within their means and they were resourceful & inspirational. Their style stays with me too, silk headscarves, framed handbags and impeccable manners. Everything a girl should have or be. Surely, they would choose a handwritten note over a text message any day of the week and twice on a Sunday? An inspiration to us all.

The best part of my job is packaging up all the orders that come in from the website. It makes me happy to know that the products I have chosen are the right ones and that there are many stationery addicts like me out there looking for a gorgeous collection of products from the best suppliers on the market. My objective is to mix the popular brands with the little known, independent suppliers all striving for the same thing – to get stylishly organised!

JULIE BRIAN
www.edieandrona.co.uk

MINDFUL
pathway
finding your way

RUTH FARENGA

Mindful Pathway

One day while working for a big IT corporation, I stared blankly at my screen...

I felt like I was looking at a brick wall; my chest was tight and I couldn't focus. I had been having panic attacks night after night coupled with really bad insomnia. It was 2012 and I was running a big Summit for 200 people out in Stockholm. It was a complex event because we collaborated with the local Ministry of Education as well as other corporates and vendors—so lots of stakeholders and important people like politicians to look after. In many ways I loved it, but, I had lots of responsibility on my shoulders. Perhaps too much (so I thought).

The cracks were starting to show.

I was experiencing anxiety and low-level depression. I felt like I couldn't cope effectively with my professional responsibilities. I had around 100 people travelling in from other countries and around 20 speakers to look after. I wanted to impress, I wanted things to be perfect but all I could do was imagine the worst possible scenarios: I was catastrophising and the smallest thing would mushroom into a massive problem in my mind. I blamed myself for lots of things and for the way I was feeling. I paid the price for that with my mental health. I tried various GPs but they only seemed interested in prescribing me drugs and finishing the appointment as quickly as possible. Therapy also didn't help me much as I wound myself in knots thinking about my problems.

Something had to change.

I had taught myself to be anxious and it was spilling over into the rest of my life too. I lived in Oxford at the time and Oxford University was already doing a lot of research and work in the area of Mindfulness.

A friend suggested I look into it. So I did. The first step was to buy a book called Mindfulness: Finding Peace in a Frantic World by Professor Mark Williams and Danny Penman. This book is now a bestseller but back then it was new. The book walked me through an 8 week Mindfulness course with a CD. I was so keen to feel better that I diligently did my meditations every day. It was a life-changing time, as a whole new perspective opened up. For the first time, I could take my foot off the accelerator and learn how to approach my negative thoughts and feelings in a different way.

I was starting to get it. My pathway had begun.

Around this time, my husband started a new job in Hertfordshire so we moved to St Albans. I was so interested in Mindfulness that I started a face-to-face 8 week Mindfulness course in London with the ELK Health Foundation. I'd started to see change in myself but I knew that more was possible.

Alongside my full-time job, I proceeded to do 2 years of teacher training on evenings and weekends to qualify as a Mindfulness teacher to teach Mindfulness-Based Cognitive Therapy (MBCT is the 8 week course format I had found so transformative).

The teacher training was a journey in itself. Over the two years our cohort evolved together, deepening our learning and sharpening our practitioner skills. We learnt self-awareness, self-discipline and self-regulation. Many people think the point of Mindfulness is to 'chill out', 'check-out' or empty your mind to reach some higher state of consciousness. Mindfulness as a secular practice is actually the opposite: meditation helps you deepen your understanding of who you really are and how you interact with the world around you.

It became clear to me that what I also got from this teacher training was a real community of like-minded people, people that wanted to be a better person each day. That was powerful.

The leap

In March 2015, the opportunity arose to venture into the unknown. Thanks to some wonderful career coaching that I also undertook at this time from a coach called Rachel Brushfield, I started to plan a varied professional life. Freelancing for a couple of charities gave me the freedom to start launching a social enterprise teaching Mindfulness: Mindful Pathway.

2015 wasn't an easy year. However, in May of that year, I went along to something called the St Albans Businesses (SABs) 'Jelly' – co-working in a pub in St Albans. It sounded random but fun! Here, I met the most wonderful business people. People who were compassionate, funny and eager to help. Through working with many other SABs, I was able to get my business off the ground: branding, website development, marketing—I was off and the first courses started in Spring 2016!

And the best bit? The courses were full! I had absolutely no idea this was going to happen. For me, this was a dream but it was also an experiment. To my amazement, the bookings started coming in and it continued that way. To this date, all the courses that we have run have been full. I employ a co-teacher on my courses and now I'm bringing in other top teachers to teach classes to both the public in St Albans and to businesses in the Southeast, London and the Midlands.

Mindfulness in the Workplace

Teaching in companies has also been eye-opening. You watch people develop and come together as teams over the duration of a course. As they develop their skills in meditation and self-awareness, their attitudes change, as do their reactions and judgements. The mood softens. People become less stressed and more at ease.

Photographs taken by
Stephanie Belton

What's really powerful is when the senior leaders of a company participate. By showing a little vulnerability, they model to the rest of the group that it's ok to feel stress and work on how best to deal with it. Company culture can develop as people are much more conscious.

The potential of community

In many ways, it still feels like early days. I have the ambition to build an urban retreat centre where people can come regularly to 'top-up' their wellbeing. Somewhere that is not only a beautiful building but also a community space. I also want to us to offer courses to disadvantaged groups who may not ordinarily have the means to participate. In the meantime, the Mindful Pathway community is growing.

We have monthly practice sessions for course graduates that are really well attended and I'm planning silent retreats for us next year.

Why Mindful Pathway?

The reason it's called Mindful Pathway is that Mindfulness is an ongoing process, not a one-off or a quick fix, but an opportunity to develop yourself day by day. The development comes from practising meditation and mindful ways of living. It also from a community of practice where you can learn from each other.

The other best bit? That others share the dream of building a community! That's been one of the most gratifying parts of it. It seems that the world needs this. People need the mental space to be able to cope with life's challenges and the support network to help them stay on their paths.

Realising my purpose in life

When I think back to how I felt 5-6 years ago, I was at my lowest point and I couldn't' see a way out. But slowly I've been able to turn my blackest moments into my dream: a social enterprise to help others on a pathway of improving their mental health and feeling happier and more fulfilled.

I feel so grateful to be where I am now.

RUTH FARENGA
www.mindfulpathway.co.uk

Photograph taken by Monir Ali

LIZ & TOMMY CAREY

Total Care Personal Training

Most of us at some point will feel that life has turned into 'Ground Hog Day' and that there is no way out. Of course, you may be happy but feel as if there is something more you want and just don't know how to grab it. Or you may lack the confidence to pursue your dreams. At these moments in time, it's important to recognise that human beings are naturally hardwired to have persistence as a default setting. Routine or structure in your life is important and can provide stability, but when it feels like you're stuck and you can't seem to fulfil your dreams then it's time to act. To get out of that cycle you've got to change how you think about change. Change, although sometimes frightening, is a good thing because it gives you the opportunity to embrace new experiences.

The idea of Total Care Personal Training is to change people and to share a way of life with YOU.

I'm Tommy, one of the founders, along with my wife Liz. I come from an acting background and Liz from marketing. We both decided that we wanted to change something and give back to the community, so this is how it all started!

One of our favourite adventure activities was snowboarding, we loved it but we wanted to enjoy it more, we needed more strength and wanted to feel good. We joined one of the BIG GYM's as you do. I started training with my wife and researching what we could do to change things around and get ready for more adventures. Then one day, and I still can't believe this happened, we were asked to leave the BIG GYM! WHY? For "Personally Training" my wife! Really?

So, having trained in conventional gyms and not really receiving the service we wanted, and with our passion for sports and living life we decided to create a unique brand that could deliver something extraordinary to people. A place that feels REAL where you can LEARN things and make new friends.

Total Care Personal Training is a unique, personal training studio in St Albans with Community at the heart. Being part of the community is something every small local business should do, get out there, speak with like-minded people and gain knowledge from everyone good and bad!

We don't just train our clients we also help out the less fortunate as well. The homeless are part of our community - if we can make a difference we will. From the very start we made sure that we became part of the community, visiting other businesses, events, charity events, networking and also encouraging collaborations with other like-minded businesses. Teaming up with Doctors, Sports Therapists and even other fitness centres. Making fitness aspirational and a part of everyday life.

Setting up community initiatives like www.therut.tv, cartoon strips to showcasing clients' results and driving a branded monster truck was getting us five consultations a week and a 95% close rate. We give great customer service with added value and have organised photo shoots, achievements, cheat/reward days and a wall of fame in the studio for clients.

I trained up and got my level three and the Amazing 12 Week Physique Certification. I was the only coach in our area that could coach this technique, giving Total Care Personal Training a competitive advantage. We teamed up with an expert body building coach, Steve Frank and mentor Nicky Sehgal (who have both run successful businesses) to advise us and be a sounding board along the way.

Nicky says "Tommy and Liz are one of the most dynamic, creative and community based business couple I have ever had the chance to work with. Their efforts go way beyond just themselves and their business. With projects like THE RUT they have brought much of the business community in St Albans together helping people change their lives."

Steve Frank, ex Body Building Coach for the Athletes South Africa said, "After 45 years in the gym industry there are very few trainers that I have met that really know what they are doing and have in my opinion have the right attitude towards training. I am extremely proud with my association with Tommy and Liz, these people have great integrity and knowledge, it doesn't hurt that they are a charming couple as well."

I have to thank my wife for inspiring me to become a Personal Trainer/Coach. Introducing me to new innovative ways of training and hooking me up with leaders in the fitness industry where I have learnt valuable techniques and skills - she now has a coach for life.

We weren't prepared for all the negativity that goes with starting your own business. "You guys must be crazy!" "It will never work." "Oh that's a recipe for a divorce." "You're both mad, look at what you have now: money, security." No one mentioned the stress, long hours not seeing each other and the hectic London life we were living.

We are not saying goodbye to our careers we are making time to enhance them and make them less stressful, working on a business that gives us our time back to do what's most important. LIVE, EXPLORE and GROW.

We have created something unique, stuck to our core values and strived to get our clients the best results possible.

We started trading Feb 21st 2015 where we opened our first studio in St Albans. We won 'New Business of the Year' from the Chamber of Commerce and the 'Federation of Small Businesses' award within the first year of trading.

What's next? Well we need to grow; not too big - just enough and keep changing, adapting and staying fresh.

If you're thinking of starting your own business then find something you are truly passionate about and set a clear goal for yourself. Find your niche and do your research on competitors in your area. Ask yourself, do you want to be working IN the business or ON the business? Then make sure you have a detailed business plan and clear vision with a five year plan, we can't stress how important this is as it keeps you more or less on track when you feel like you're getting lost!

Never quit, if you do stumble get back up and on track! Follow those dreams and goals and have fun along the way. Finally, remember to LIVE!

TOMMY & LIZ CAREY
www.tcpt.co.uk

AARTI PARMAR
AARTI PARMAR Brand Communications

AP Brand Communications

When I was 22, I set off for the Far East in search of adventure and a challenge. Fresh out of university and with a degree in Visual Communication Design (specialising in Graphic Design) in my pocket, I earmarked one year to experience new things, work hard and open my eyes to the world.

I returned ten years later, having ambitiously (but not without trepidation) grabbed an opportunity to partner with some people in Kuala Lumpur and run a creative agency.

It was a rollercoaster ride that taught me so much. I was exposed to the pressure of pitching, growing a team, being challenged daily, hitting glass ceilings, dealing with empty promises, adapting to big egos (and little ones), working with different cultures and ethics... but above all producing brilliant creative work that made a difference.

Without knowing it at the time, I was on an amazing journey, sharpening the tools of my trade with every step.

Immediately after I returned home from Malaysia 2011, I spent 3 years managing the design, marketing and communications for our family business. In comparison to many of the big accounts I had previously worked on, this business came with a shoe-string budget.

Nevertheless, with some creative thinking, I successfully managed to increase awareness, footfall and sales. It made me realise that not every business has the cash, know-how, time or resources to manage their design and marketing, but with the right help it can be done. And done really well. I have seen how the creation of a strong brand can help a business to see clearly, feel stronger and shout louder. With my breadth of design, branding, marketing and commercial experience, I felt I was equipped to offer a multi-faceted service to small businesses who needed support. And so....AP Brand Communications was born.

Managing everything in a business, you suddenly become the admin, accountant, marketer, and in my case, designer. Overtime I overcame this by sourcing some of these things out. Allowing me space to enjoy what I love doing!

My biggest achievements have been:

- Having lots of one to ones over the years. Building lovely relationships whom I now use for my own business, refer to my clients, friends and family. And have business referred to me.

- Being selected as a finalist for Best Women Business Awards in the Business Services category.

- Being selected as a finalist for St Albans Chamber of Commerce awards in New Business category. Pleasantly surprised and chuffed to be nominated for this one.

- Presented a SAB (St Albans Businesses) Woohoo Awards for dream achiever and collaborator. Lovely to be nominated and recognised by other businesses.

- Diploma in Personal Performance Coaching (Distinction) – Effective tool set to use when I'm providing business brand consultation and brand discovery sessions for my clients. Also to use outside of business.

- Selected to sit on the board for STANTA – St Albans Enterprise Agency. – Allowing me to broaden my knowledge, exposure, and actively be part of a successful agency.

- Firewalking on coals that were 2000 degrees hot!! An empowering experience that helped remove mental obstacles, supercharge the mind, and left me with a renewed confidence in myself. Awesome experience!!!

The most fulfilling thing for me is helping my clients to connect with their business. Being part of their business brand journey, and seeing them come out the other end with a brand they love, and are connected to, and can proudly and confidently say this is who we are.

- Meeting amazing, inspiring, eclectic mix of people and mindsets.

- Knowing there is no limit to what you can achieve!

- Freedom and flexibility.

My life has changed since I started my business. You never switch off for a start!

Realise the importance of your time, and have more value for it.

I get to meet many entrepreneurs and I love hearing their stories; why they're doing what they're doing, how they got there, their passion, their successes and their challenges. All the things that drive people to strive for more, for better.

Every person behind a business is different, even if the product or service offering is just the same as the competition. What drives me is being able to bring out that difference. I consider this to be the heart and mind of a business. It's my job to capture it, design it and communicate it. I like listening to people and building positive, impactful relationships that go the distance. By doing so, I feel I am better able to deliver a brand that feels right and has real meaning.

What would I say to anyone who is thinking of starting their own business?

Apart from the obvious of doing the market research, business plan, vision etc, I would say having abundance of passion, persistence and enthusiasm is key!! Know your WHY. In times of challenges and adversities, this will be a driving factor on overcoming and moving things forward, and ultimately enjoy what you are doing.

Not everything has to be perfect when you start, it's a journey of learning, discovering, exploring and improving. Enjoy it!! Remember, 'the journey of a thousand miles begins with one step'.

Surround yourself with like-minded people that can support you and vice versa. Networking groups are great for this.

Network!! Build relationships, this builds trust and credibility. People do business with people who they know like, and trust. Surround yourself with people who have dreams, desire, and ambition; they'll help you push for and realise your own :)

AARTI PARMAR
www.aartiparmar.com

SUSAN HEATON-WRIGHT

ExecutiveVoice Executive Voice
Vocal and Communications Training

I had my son and gave up my career as a professional opera singer. Motherhood resulted in me meeting lots of different people (no longer from the opera/classical industry) and I was constantly being asked how I projected my voice; delivered presentations; managing fear and nerves. I realized there was a need for this skill set, given my professional experience as a performer and particularly as a voice expert. As I am a former teacher (QTS), I had experience and qualifications in training for a business and teaching. I spent some time discovering what potential clients needed: what were their pain points and how my experience and expertise could support them to be the very best version of themselves in a variety of business situations. As well as speaking and presenting, I also developed skills and knowledge for non-verbal communication and listening skills and expanded my knowledge of developing confidence, mindset, managing nerves and self-evaluation through studying. I have built up my expertise through experience and developing confidence.

One of the biggest struggles at first was to differentiate from singing teaching. Initially I called myself a 'voice coach' and of course some people thought I taught singing or that I would get them to sing! As I haven't worked in the corporate sector, but my target market is there, I have had to work hard to "Speak their language" and understand the buying structure and journey so that my service appeals to them directly. I also struggled to set the pricing for my services, and continue to have advice and review them.

It is fantastic when I see or hear one of my clients being interviewed on the TV or radio; knowing that I have supported them in their journey to success. I have been invited to speak internationally on being a great communicator and am regularly interviewed on radio, international podcasts and webinars as well as speaking at conferences, professional organisations and in businesses. It is great to be considered an expert!

I am regularly 'found' by individuals seeking help, as well as being recommended to work with very senior people in multi-national organisations. The REAL achievement is that as a schoolgirl I really struggled with speaking in public and got terribly nervous, and I went from this to being a soloist, performing in front of 3000 + audiences. My personal journey has enabled me to understand and empathize with my clients, particularly when they feel nervous, ignored or undervalued.

My successes are due to my own hard work, expertise and talent. There is something really special saying and admitting this in public! I have pushed myself outside my comfort zone, and I have experienced situations and met people I would never have had the opportunity to meet otherwise. I often meet very successful, senior individuals within large organisations, and I get to support and help them. BRILLIANT! I have had to do things I initially found very scary: writing a blog, recording my podcast and VLOG and even public speaking – and now I'm the joint president of the Professional Speaking Association in the Eastern region. That wouldn't have happened if I wasn't running my business. My life has changed in many positive ways.

I have been able to create a business around my son. When he was younger I only worked a few hours a week and now he's 17

I am working much longer hours. I have certainly become more assertive and aware of the value of my expertise and time.

My motivation is all about the client. I really want to support individuals and teams to be the best communicators they can be and present the best versions of themselves in business situations. When I start working with a new client, I genuinely want to share skills and confidence so they will become more visible, confident and heard. When I hear their good news stories – and I keep in touch with many of my clients, it inspires me to find more clients to work with.

To anyone thinking of staring their own business, I would say, be brave; there are "Ups and Downs". Be prepared to ask others for advice, either in an online group or a regular meeting group (such as the St Albans Business Group and the Jellies). Ensure you set up a good book keeping process from the beginning as well as any specific legal contracts and insurance. I know this sounds boring, but it will protect you and your business. Spend some time considering what the values and aims are of your business, as these are your brand not the colour of your logo.

SUSAN HEATON-WRIGHT
www.executivevoice.co.uk

LOUISE MURPHY
Captain Tortue

Little did I realise that my life would come full circle! When I was 16, I took my first Saturday job working in the women's fashion shop "Richards" and I absolutely loved it. Today, and several years later, I am running my own business with Captain Tortue, selling stylish French ladies fashions from home. Maybe it had something to do with my love of clothes, love of France and desire to run my own business. Actually, it was a coincidence and a chance conversation that led to where I am today, but however I got here, it is a dream coming true!

Having graduated with a degree in Management Studies and French in 1992, I had hoped to land a French-speaking role in a glamorous business. Instead I earnt a place on a management training scheme with Mobil Oil...not the glamour life I had hoped for! That said, my 10 years at Mobil and, later BP, allowed me to experience a variety of roles in sales, marketing, communications, events, and team management – all invaluable in developing my own business today.

At the end of my maternity leave, I decided I wanted some time to be a Mum. After a few years, I took on a part-time sales and marketing role for a local company but I never felt truly satisfied. I had secretly always harboured a desire to run my own business; I could just never work out what I was going to do, if I had the "guts" to do it, or how it was going to fit it into family life!

So I started to investigate "buying into" a business instead. After lots of research and chats with friends about opportunities, a very good friend said, "You should do Captain Tortue, you'd be great at it!" I wasn't immediately convinced, but a week later I went out for dinner with two girlfriends and I commented on the tops they were both wearing; both different; both from Captain Tortue.

And the rest is history! The following day, I was on the phone to the local consultant (and my now wonderful manager). A week later, I was attending the launch of the Autumn/Winter collections and a week after that I was a Style Consultant and business owner with Captain Tortue, full of excitement and enthusiasm for the journey ahead.

Captain Tortue is a direct-selling business and I had my hesitations about entering "this world". I'm not a natural "salesperson" and "sales" definitely does not sit in my comfort zone! So I had to find a way of selling that worked for me. It helps that the clothes are great, as they sell themselves, but I still had to get myself in front of people. After a while, I discovered that it didn't really feel like I was selling. What I enjoyed was providing a service to help women save time and money by shopping from home and to help them look and feel better about themselves, whatever their shape or size, by offering personal style advice. This, I could do!

One of the factors in my decision to join Captain Tortue was the ability to be my own boss and work flexible hours. I was also motivated by the fact that I would be directly rewarded for my efforts in cash and clothes (so now I'm making money and spending less, but my wardrobe is full!). I work around family life and put as much time and effort in as I chose. As an "all-or-nothing" girl, I tend to throw myself into things and will often take on too much; so knowing when to say 'no, thank you' and staying focused are areas I need to work on.

A key lesson that I have learnt is to write down my goals; it really is helping to keep me on track.

In the early days, I worried about succeeding – Would I have any customers? Would anyone like the clothes? Could I really do it? Before going for it with Captain Tortue, I asked many questions to seek the reassurance I needed: Is it a quality brand? Is it financially secure? Is there any training/support? Is my financial risk low/affordable? What are the rewards? Then it was over to me to make it a success.

In hindsight, my worries were unnecessary; I saw amazing results in my very first season and achieved the accolade of Top New Consultant in the UK. My sales continue to grow; my customer base is expanding and the customer feedback I receive is really rewarding. And to top it all, in 2017 I started to build my own team of consultants and received a promotion. The future looks exciting!

As much as I enjoy the financial rewards and the free clothes, I am particularly motivated by seeing my business grow and thrive. I get huge amounts of satisfaction from my customers who tell me they love the clothes and the service I provide and every time I get a new customer, I have an extra spring in my step!

Since my business began in 2016, I have experienced things I had never even dreamt about! This includes being a catwalk model for Captain Tortue UK; modelling for a local photographer re-designing her new website; attending numerous networking events (who even knew these existed?) and meeting lots of customers and business owners with many developing into great friendships. I have learnt new skills, pushed myself out of my comfort zone and grown my confidence and self-esteem.

Finally, as a Mum to two teenage girls, I hope I am showing them how you can be a mother and a business owner with ambition... fingers crossed I am getting the balance right!

I CAN. I WILL. END OF STORY.

LOUISE MURPHY
www.facebook.com/LouiseMurphy
CaptainTortue/

SARAH WREN

Hertfordshire Independent Living Service (HILS)

I joined HILS in June 2010 as Chief Executive, having led the organisation as founder Chairman from its incorporation. Prior to joining HILS I worked as a lecturer on a business and management degree programme, and held a number of chairmanships in local charitable organisations. I have strived to make a positive contribution to my community throughout my working life, and as an advocate of the principles of a social enterprise, I was keen to take on a new challenge.

I first decided to get involved with HILS because I hoped that my determination and genuine desire to change things for the better would enable me to lead and develop the company, with a passion to see it succeed and fulfil a wider social role.

My role involves developing the business to provide excellent services, value for money for the public purse, and flexible local employment opportunities. I am also proud to lead a caring and committed team of people who are passionate about serving people and changing the world for the better.

How we started

Before 2007, meals on wheels in Hertfordshire was a bit of a postcode lottery; depending on where you lived, there was a different service, price, and food. So, in 2007 Hertfordshire County Council established our social enterprise, originally named Hertfordshire Community Meals, to create a fairer meals on wheels service for people in Hertfordshire.

From small beginnings...

We began with just one site in Letchworth; two vehicles, seven staff, and a team of volunteers delivering meals in the North Hertfordshire district.

Great things grow!

By 2013, the remaining nine Hertfordshire districts had transferred their clients to us, and four sites were established across the county; in Hemel Hempstead, Letchworth, St Albans, and Ware. We still operate out of these four sites today.

In April 2015, our name was changed and we began operating as Hertfordshire Independent Living Service. This new name is much more fitting, as it reflects all we do, which is more than just delivering meals! Our other services are also aimed at helping elderly and vulnerable people to stay independent, and to provide support. For example, we offer pop-in visits to people's homes, installing and maintaining alarms and telecare, and running dementia fun clubs. In the coming years, we also plan to continue to develop these services even further.

Over the years the company has expanded and we now employ over 200 people and deliver around 500,000 meals and friendly welfare checks every year. We see up to 2,000 clients every day, and offer a 365-day service across the county.

Bucking national trends

Over the intervening ten years however, it hasn't all been plain sailing. We've faced some real challenges; particularly when money is tight in health and social care, and when lots of other meals on wheels services have been axed. Despite budget cuts, HILS is unusual not least because we have bucked the trend in a declining meals on wheels market, and are now the largest social enterprise of its kind in the UK.

We remain one of the few meals on wheels services to be expanding, with just 17% of councils in the South East providing meals on wheels. We've weathered the storms, we've got through it, and we've changed almost every part of our operation so that we can be more cost effective and provide an excellent and caring service to thousands more people.

Our Approach and Ethos

As a charitable social enterprise, we trade to do good and support people, reinvesting any surplus into helping our clients. We believe in paying people a fair wage, and all of our staff are paid at least the Living Wage Foundation's Living Wage. We use paid staff to deliver our meals, and volunteers provide vital support to deliver some of our other services, like the dementia fun clubs. We also believe in helping people back into work. A number of our staff have found it difficult to work for a wide range of reasons and we have helped them to thrive in the workplace with training and support.

Our values are central to everything we do. They tell you what to expect from us, and they tell all our team members what to expect from each other. People have high expectations

of our work, and our values reflect that; we aim to be caring, have good communication, be community focused, be conscientious, cost efficient and creative.

Our St Albans Site

Our most unusual site is in St Albans, based at the Jubilee Centre on Catherine Street. Here we deliver meals on wheels and also provide a community hub, with a dementia fun club offering an exciting mix of activities run by highly trained staff and volunteers on week days. A drop in restaurant with discounted prices for elderly people, serving hot lunchtime meals and desserts every week day, and there are also rooms for hire for community groups, private events, or meetings – seven days a week!

Our Impact

Our biggest achievements, and what has always motivated the business and those working for HILS, are the clients we serve, and seeing the benefit our service has brought to them.

In 2016, our client survey revealed the impact we have had, including making people's lives easier, giving their families greater peace of mind, making them feel happier, helping them to stay living at home, helping them feel better nourished and more independent, less lonely, faster to recover from ill-health or personal difficulty and have even managed to help clients so much that their visits to their GP have decreased.

Our people and teams are the things which make us really special. Making sure that we all believe, and really live our values, is crucial. Any time one of our team members goes out and about, and speaks to the people that we're serving, they are really taking warmth, and goodness, and happiness with them, trying to impact people's lives for the better.

Here at HILS, we aspire to change the world – starting in Hertfordshire!

SARAH WREN

www.hertsindependentliving.org

JENNY SOPPET-SMITH

 Digital Jen

The DigitalJen business story is one that is a bit like the business itself – formed of lots of elements that have combined into a single entity. Having my own business wasn't really in 'the plan' – although I'm still not entirely sure what 'the plan' was then or is now. That probably isn't the best start for a piece by a business consultant who talks about plans, goals and getting your business where you want it to be. Let me explain...

I trained as a musician – specialising in trumpet and piano performance and something called musicology – which some people find very interesting and some don't. What it does do though is make you look at all the detail, all the time. I had been plagued with ill health through my secondary school career and my time at university was no different, with major surgery in my first year, slipped discs in my second and more surgery in my third. I graduated in 1996, unable to get a place to train as a teacher due to my health and set off work in London – where the streets weren't paved with gold or arts administration jobs that paid enough to live on.

Fast forward a few years of a variety of jobs in a variety of industries – all focussing on customer service, operations management and elements of IT as it developed at the time. Ill health had continued to be a major factor of my life but with

no medical professional able to diagnose what the actual problem was.

I didn't return to work after the birth of my daughter in 2005 and had my son in 2007. After he was born I received the diagnosis that explained all my medical problems – I have a type of Ehlers Danlos Syndrome. Although I then knew what caused the problems, I also knew it couldn't be fixed. My son wasn't a particularly healthy baby – and I had a toddler in tow – work was the last thing on my mind.

For a variety of reasons, we became a Homestart family. On one visit our volunteer opened the conversation with "I know this isn't really the right time in your life for this... but I think I've found you a job". That was the Monday. I had an interview on the Thursday and started 'for a couple of weeks on a self-employed basis' the following Monday. Again, fast forward 3.5 years plagued with more surgery, ill health and trying to juggle two children with what were becoming more complex medical and behavioural needs and holding down a job wasn't sustainable. I went out on my own.

The business grew by word of mouth recommendations. I already had a successful blog on Wordpress and was becoming more and more fascinated by the platform. I had properly discovered my inner geek – and a real love of photography. My initial idea was to offer Wordpress website design, blogger outreach, writing blogs for businesses and photography. I went to my first St Albans Businesses Jelly – confused everyone with my then business name and wondered whether I was grown up enough for this world of networking and success.

Rapidly approaching 40, I was then involved in an accident on an escalator in London. Time for a major rethink on everything.

Work, family, home, priorities – the whole lot. In the 8 months following that accident things changed – both in terms of getting out there with work, but also my focus on what I wanted to do. Having a business that meant I could be using my skills, making a living and able to attend the ever increasing number of medical and educational appointments my children needed was the goal. Blogger outreach wasn't what people wanted but my WordPress and consultancy skills were.

The business name still wasn't right – and over a cuppa with a client I discussed the fact the name needed to change but I didn't know what to.

"It's obvious!" came the reply (cue blank look from me...)

You ARE just Digital Jen. You do things digitally, it's a bit clever because you're the digital generation and it's easy to remember. It stuck.

An old friend designed the logo, I put a website together, I tentatively mentioned the name change at the next Jelly I went to and I was convinced there and then it was absolutely the right choice. I had a brand, I had a set of values and I had a plan.

As I write, it's nearly two and a half years since I fell down that escalator. Rapidly approaching two years of being Digital Jen. The business has grown phenomenally – I think through sticking to my values (be kind, be helpful, be honest, be nice, be involved), changing 'the plan' constantly and by being part of the St Albans Business Community.

As Ruth Farenga from the Mindful Pathway said on LinkedIn; "this woman has grown a digital communications business with a difference - ethical but cuts to the chase"

It's a brilliant summary of what we do. Because now it is a 'we' – the wonderful Natalie Atkins joined the team at the beginning of 2017, enabling the business to offer more services, better support and for my plan of having strong processes and controls in place that underpin the business to come to fruition.

Going forwards, the plan is to keep adapting to what our clients need and want. The world of business is constantly changing, as is the digital environment. The needs of my family are changing too – and they must be an integral part of my business model, as does endeavouring to keep myself as healthy as possible.

What's the long-term plan? To keep being ethical, fair and open. If that means we turn down some work, we'll turn it down. If that means we grow – brilliant. If we continue in a sustainable model and our clients are delighted with what we do, our families are thriving and we are well – that is just as brilliant.

What's the short-term plan? Probably another cup of tea and having a chat about what we need to do next.

JENNY SOPPET-SMITH
www.digitaljen.co.uk

MATT DAWSON
Inspire Music School

The decision to start Inspire Music School was like most businesses, more influenced by events and circumstances rather than a conscious decision.

The story of how the school got established actually begins way back when I worked in sales. Needless to say I was growing rapidly more and more bored and frustrated working in the predictable 9-5 sort of environment. My wife encouraged me to go after a job in music as that was the area that I had studied for years but as many may or may not know, it's quite hard to make a decent living in music. I started teaching guitar as a tutor and realised very quickly that I had a pretty decent knack for teaching others. From there I progressed into secondary schools becoming a resident guitar teacher. I guess you could say it was at this time that 'I learnt my trade' and was making a living from it!

I landed in St Albans after getting a contract to teach in a local guitar school. It was here that I learnt how to teach to larger groups and classes. My students were quickly coming up the ranks as the higher performers and eventually I was made the manager of the school. It became my role to oversee the teaching by myself and other teachers as well as handle all the cogs that made the school tick over throughout the week.

On the second of December in 2016 I had my monthly Skype meeting with my Director to talk about the progress for that month. It was here that he landed the bombshell that he wished to close the school. In my opinion this was totally the wrong decision and all that was needed to keep us open was a bit of elbow grease and time. I was faced with possibly one of the most daunting decisions I've ever had to face. Start my own school as a limited company and go into business for myself as Director or sink back into the dreaded 9-5 and go back to a 'real job'. I had to make the choice and the clock was ticking as the closing date got nearer.

Once the students were informed I was left with a group of students that weren't willing to give up - however I had nowhere to teach, no educational material and no equipment. The decision was made to take the leap of faith and start my own school. I had two months to learn what a limited company was, draft up a teaching programme, secure a teaching space whilst instilling a sense of calm in our client base. The best part of it was all our clients were cheering me on! On the 12th of February all the teachers went their own ways along with all the equipment and materials and on the 13th we opened with all new logo's, website, syllabus work and equipment. After my first week I looked back and gave myself a rather nice pat on the back whilst thinking 'not bad for a kitchen salesman without a maths GCSE'. I wanted a seamless transition from one school to the next and managed to pull it off. As a school, we've gone from strength to strength ever since.

Running my own business has come with its own struggles however, one of the main ones is myself. As a first time business owner I often am faced with feelings of being well out my depth. I sit down at the start of the week and think, 'wait, don't people have to study business at college and uni in order to do this?!?'. As I had very little experience in the start I was always worried about getting it wrong or making a wrong move. I would think 'I know mistakes are all part of it, but mistakes are expensive so I'd rather avoid them' so I would often play it safe and get nowhere. I only really saw any momentum when I started to just go for it and take risks and really just get out there.

To date, my biggest achievement would be defining the new culture within our school. Me and my long term students went through a lot in the start. I had to show them that I was capable of leading the new school and taking us to where we needed to go. Naturally they had doubts as to if I could complete the tasks required to get us going. I assured them that all was in hand. I made the conscious decision to put our students at the centre of everything we did. The monetary rewards would now be a result of the quality work that we were going to do and not the goal forsaking everything else. I wanted an almost cult like following of students who were loyal because they knew we cared about them learning the guitar and not just after their fee's. Through the drastic reductions in student turnover it's safe to say we achieved the new culture I was after.

Things are different in every way for me after taking the leap to go into business. As well as being newly married and a massive change in job I'm sure you can imagine the amount of plate spinning that has had to take place. My biggest change has been in myself really. I've had to become far more disciplined around work. Not to resist slacking off and being lazy but actually intentionally create boundaries where I will not work. I'm a person that can obsess and just keep working so by putting a start and stop time on things I'm more productive, happy and able to focus my attention on everything in my life correctly.

As per the name, inspiring is the game. I need to stay inspired as sometimes it can feel like a hamster wheel scenario. I look at the positive impact we have in our community. We give lessons to those with learning difficulties, build relationships with teens struggling with exams and teach those in their 80's - to name a few groups of people. All of the above receive a skill which has been a huge benefit and comfort and this thought is what keeps me going on those slow and slightly uninspiring days.

My main advice for those that are wanting to go into business is just go for it. Have a vision and step towards it. There are so many people that are afraid to try and settle for the minimum cliché boring life. Don't become one of those people, keep going and never give up even when the work day is a tough one. On these days it's important to remember what Einstein said and it's words our students live by, 'You never fail until you stop trying'.

MATT DAWSON
www.inspiremusicschool.com/

DEBBIE STEWART
TimeOut4Me

My story starts in 1992, just after my first son was born, with a company called Nutrimetics. I joined and trained as a bridal make-up artist using their organic skincare and cosmetics range.

This was ideal, as it gave me the flexibility to work from home and bring up my baby. Clients would come to me for consultations during the evening and my husband would care for our son on the weekends while I was working. This was a lovely job as I was always working within the happy and exciting atmosphere surrounding a bride-to- be – opening the door to florists, seeing the brides in their wedding dresses.

In 1996 our second son was born and completed our family. From this, I progressed to pamper parties for children, still working with Nutrimetics but introducing home-made face masks and hand scrubs.

In 2002, I discovered the wonderful healing energy of Reiki as a patient, and then decided to train as a Reiki Practitioner, whilst at the same time studying to become a Bach Flower Practitioner. This period was particularly stressful for me due to family issues. I needed something to support me. These two therapies have been an enormous help in growing my confidence and strength, and have supported me in very stressful personal situations. It was a huge joy, as a mother, to be able to offer these to my young family and friends, and in turn to see them benefit from them. My pamper parties grew to be more holistic as I introduced more of these therapies.

Once both of my sons were at school I knew that I wanted to help other mums. Not everyone has family and support around them. I wrote to the local hospital explaining my experience and that I wanted to volunteer my services as a holistic therapist. As a result of this a lead health visitor in Hertsmere invited me to join their weekly 'Health and Harmony' sessions for women who were displaying post- natal stress and depression. I particularly remember one mum with a six-week- old baby saying she felt that she had "been put back together again" after a Reiki treatment.

I can still remember today how I felt after that first session. I was bubbling with so much happiness and gratitude, and walking to collect my sons from school afterwards, I felt like skipping all the way. This was when I really felt that this was the work that I passionately wanted to develop and continue.

Sadly, lack of funding put a halt to these amazing sessions.

From there, in 2005 I became a Home-Start volunteer. Home-Start is one of the leading family support charities in the UK, helping families with children under five years old deal with whatever life throws at them. I undertook an eight-week training course before I was assigned to my first Family. I met so many lovely families during my time with Home-Start, each with their own individual challenges. I am still in contact with some of them, as a friend, after all these years. During this time a health visitor, (now a very good friend), was invited to Home- Start to deliver a parenting course to its volunteers, the idea being to pass this knowledge on to the Home-Start families. I was totally hooked, and loved this course and the notion of supporting other families. The health visitor also remarked that I would make an excellent Parenting course facilitator. So I embarked on the next stage of my development and after several training courses and exams I qualified as a Parenting Practitioner in 2007.

At a Home-Start volunteers' day, the guest speaker was Robert Holden, founder of The Happiness Project, (which looks at opening up new ways of looking at our lives and becoming the most vibrant, happy, alive versions of ourselves). I was so inspired by Robert's teachings that, in 2005 I enrolled on his eight-week programme, followed by a five–day 'Coaching Happiness' course in 2010.

Meditation has been part of my daily life for many years, and I wanted to incorporate it into my work. I attended the eight week Mindfulness Course (designed by Jon Kabat-Zinn), in 2008 - the aim being to learn new ways to handle challenging physical sensations, feelings, moods or social interactions Over the past ten years I have been fortunate to deliver many parenting courses and wellbeing sessions at Children's Centres around Hertfordshire, which I find extremely rewarding.

I launched TimeOut4Me in 2012 to encapsulate all of my experience in order to deliver Parenting and Wellbeing sessions and courses working with parents on ways to connect more deeply with their children and recapture the magic and joys of being a parent/child. The biggest thing that your children want is your time. We advise and support to explore and encourage parents' strengths for themselves to enable them to be the best parent they can be, helping to build up confidence as a parent and their opinions of themselves whilst recognizing that every parent is unique and has different ways of bringing up their children. "There is more harmony in the household and less stress"

My varied training, experience and passion enables me to offer a wide range of services.

My aims are to help others enjoy life to the full and make the most of and appreciate every day. We all need to make time for ourselves so that we can recharge our batteries.

Having fun and memory-making days with laughter is always a wonderful way to look back at your childhood.

I am so proud of many things, but in my opinion nothing beats the privilege of being a mother, watching our children grow into happy and independent individuals.

DEBBIE STEWART
www.facebook.com/
DebbieTimeOut4Me/

my mustard

PAY PER CLICK ADVERTISING AGENCY

JUNE CORY

My Mustard

I was fed up working for people who didn't care about people.

Fed up of only talking to clients who had complaints.

I believe if you treat your staff like royalty they will treat your customers like royalty.

Always loved selling advertising – you give me a quid and you make a tenner, what's not to like?

I like learning new things. Beware the closed mind.

We got a letter when we'd been going about two months saying 83% of businesses fail! I keep it on my noticeboard along with a photocopy of the first cheque we received for invoice MM001. Thanks David.

I am massively interested in what people do and how they make a living. Nosy, is the word.

Stumbled across an article about Google AdWords in 2006, what if I hadn't?

Business plan on back of fag packet. Literally.

BT nearly broke me – no phones for three weeks in my first month of trading. Serious tears were shed.

Had enough money to pay my employee and my mortgage for three months. If I failed I'd get another job.

It took until Year 5 not to worry about money and I still keep a really tight rein on cashflow.

We were almost called Kipper. I know, I know....

Turnover is vanity, profit is sanity, cash is king.

Look at the Flat Rate VAT scheme.

Get a really good accountant.

Took the best bits from corporate life – appraisals, structure, bold forecasts - and left the rubbish – politics, reports about what went wrong, bcc memos.

Fell in love with networking.

I truly believe in Givers Gain and whilst BNI has its detractors I learned so much in my 18 months at Chariots Chapter.

It was a man's world in 2007 and to an extent it still is.

I never ever discount.

I am very lucky. And the harder I worked the luckier I become.

I have had maybe five or six days in ten years that I wanted to work for somebody else.

I don't stop when I'm tired, I stop when I'm done.

Linked In is the best network online for business.

Dream big.

Be loyal.

Manage your own expectations first, then manage theirs.

There is plenty of business for everyone.

I have a Nine Poke Rule. Call me for more details....

ABC – Always Be Closing

I am inspired by the spirit and vision of other people.

Measure the input not the output.

Media Understanding, Sales Training, Advertising Response, Done.

Watch every penny but when you want something, get the best.

Catch your staff doing something right.

I am the UK's most formidable List Writer.

Reward them regularly.

I still use a Page To A Day diary – so sue me.....

Never ever ever give up.

Start with the end in mind.

Only do what only you can do. (Thanks Carl.)

Surround yourself with people smarter than you.

Don't pay for sick leave.

Be bold.

Get an apprentice – my girl is the absolute nuts.

Know your weaknesses and play to your strengths.

Be authentic.

Be yourself, everyone else is taken.

Eat. The. Frog.

Paperless office? Ha!

Make your default position positive and your energy level high.

Do what you say you're going to do.

Find your voice and use it.

I am constantly surprised by how brilliant people can be.

I am late. All the time. It is a major failing of us optimists.

Vive la difference – celebrate opposite points of view.

Put the VAT aside.

Everything is hard before it's easy.

Have a Plan B.

Do the same type of tasks together – it's a Right Brain, Left Brain thing.

Smile when you dial.

I am a repeat offender hotel stationery thief. Sorry.

Never go networking and say, "I don't want business". It's the only thing we'll remember.

Have a truly memorable 60 seconds.

Know your customers.

Know your customer's customers.

Drag people screaming out of their comfort zones; they will amaze you and themselves.

Buy Local.

And don't haggle it's deeply unattractive.

Ask LOTS of open questions:

I KEEP six honest serving-men (They taught me all I knew); Their names are What and Why and When and How and Where and Who.

Pay your bills on time.

Expect Nothing. Blame No one, Do Something.

"You MUST have a Facebook page." No, you don't.

How do you eat an elephant? Bite by bite.

This is not an act, I really am this optimistic.

"You were born with two ears and one mouth for a reason, so that we can listen twice as much as we speak." It's a work in progress......

Don't expect anyone to love your business like you do – that is not how it works

Chase debt hard. It is literally your businesses' lifeblood

If you want a pay rise, your need a rate increase.

It takes as much effort to sell a £30 ad as it does to sell a £3000 one.

Use social media – find your space and work it every day.

When something scares you bite its head off.

Share knowledge, go on.... Scatter that wisdom.

Learn patience..... the phone rang the other day and it was someone I pitched to seven years ago. Seven bloody years. (Yes, I got the business.)

Nail your USP early on.

Get people to challenge you.

Admit when you're wrong.

Work Life balance? Ask someone else I am rubbish at it!

Pay it forward.

"You MUST have an exit strategy." No, you don't.

Live your brand all day every day.

Ask for help, people LOVE to help.

Keep It Simple.

"If you don't do it excellently, don't do it at all. Because if it's not excellent, it won't be profitable or fun, and if you're not in business for fun or profit, what the hell are you doing there?" Robert Townsend

JUNE CORY
www.mymustard.co.uk

BEN SCHNEIDER

BLS COMPUTER SOLUTIONS **BLS Computer Solutions**

I decided that I wanted to start my own business in November 2012 after getting inundated with a number of requests for help to fix computer issues by neighbours and friends. At the time, I was working as a technician providing IT support for a school and could see that politics and personalities distracted me from getting the job done: I just wanted to provide the best solution in an efficient, simple and honest manner.

Dave (dad) had just left a software company after 16 years having worked as a programmer, project leader and latterly working in IT support.

I believed that together we could form a great partnership: I'd been into tech since I got my first (shared) PC and PDA and therefore knew what people were using their tech for, and why, whereas Dave had the corporate and business experience.

We both agreed that we wanted to become a company that really served our customers – treat them as we would want to be treated, which is timely, appropriately and caringly.

We started off in shared offices with WENTA which supports start-up businesses. This was invaluable – getting business advice and being able to learn off other start-ups as well as developing some great working relationships with the other businesses. Back then all we had was 2 school size lockers and 2 hot desks which were first come first served.

When faced with a quandary, we try to think as if we are the customer – communication is paramount and of course deadlines too, which is something that we are still learning to master – ensuring that we understand the exact importance of requests so that we can accurately schedule the work in.

It's been a great achievement from initially working at home to renting a 500-square foot office by effectively growing the business by acquiring customers primarily by word of mouth - it really does reflect our ethos.

It's gratifying to know that I am free to do what I want when I want (with obvious constraints) and that I am free to offer customers the personal and consistent service we pride ourselves in giving.

I want to carry on growing the business as much as possible by referrals however I realise that we can't and shouldn't do everything ourselves, another lesson learnt, and therefore look forward to working with external companies as part of our success. On a personal note, my first luxury item will be an Audi A5 with a personal number plate of BLS 4 IT.

BEN SCHNEIDER
www.blscomputersolutions.co.uk

LUCY HOLLIDAY

Nicola Holliday Foundation

I am setting up a foundation in memory of my mother who died from inflammatory breast cancer in July 2014. I am a professional fundraiser and I was racking my brains about ways to honour her memory in a way that she would have supported. My mother was a strong character, but a private and modest person, so it was difficult to find the right solution to uphold her. In recent years, I have been a bid writer for several charities and I have been a keen fundraiser for most of my life! I am setting up a foundation in memory of mummy to raise funds to support people with life-limiting illnesses and their families.

At mummy's funeral, we suggested donations to either Cancer Research UK or Salisbury Hospice, the place where mummy spent her final days. I wanted to find something that was a tribute specifically for her, something that would have met with her approval, understated, but not insignificant. A tough ask. I know that she would never have approved of a bench regardless of the location. I thought about a tree, as she loved nature and wildlife, but this did not seem quite right either.

My mother comes from a family rich in heritage, half Australian and half Orthodox Jew, she is a direct descendant of George Wyndham, a top level English cricketer who emigrated to Australia in the early nineteenth century. George settled in the Hunter Valley and became a farmer, wine-

grower and pastoralist. Wyndham Estate is still a thriving vineyard and we enjoyed their wine at my wedding nine years ago!

My grandfather was one of eight children and became a radio engineer in the Australian Air Force. He came over to the UK in the 1930's to study Radio Engineering at the University of Cambridge. During this period, he met my grandmother, Esther Goldberg, the daughter of a member of the Merchant Navy. Esther was an Orthodox Jew and married my grandfather on the condition that she forsook her religion. My mother was born in Australia in 1940. She lived there until 1941, when my grandfather was posted back to the UK to help the allies during World War II. When my father and I were sorting out my mother's belongings, we found the tag, which my mother wore when she was on board the vessel that transported her family back to the UK, a journey that took about 6 weeks.

Throughout her childhood, my mother's family moved every few years, following the Royal Air Force postings. My grandparents had four daughters, my mother being the oldest, closely followed by Beverley, Isla and then Carolyn. The majority of the postings were in South West England and also included a period in France towards the end of the 1940's.

From the age of ten, my mother went to the Godolphin in Salisbury, Wiltshire, to prevent too much disruption to her education. My mother had a very positive experience at boarding school and spoke fondly of her time there: she became Captain of the lacrosse team, a giddy sporting height which I never reached!

My parents met on the ski slopes in Switzerland and settled in Surrey, where both my brother and I were born. My father is a chemist who pursued a career in patents and we lived in Munich for 14 years, where he was a judge in the European Patent Office.

My parents retired to Wiltshire, just over the hill from George Wyndham's house in 1995. My mother was very involved in many aspects of village life – one of our neighbours called her a 'force for good' when she died. Mummy was one of the most selfless and giving people, always striving for the best and helping people and organisations. She continued with some of her voluntary work. My mother looked after herself so well, embracing super foods and vegetarianism, decades before they became universally popular. She never smoked, barely drank alcohol and was extremely fit throughout her life. Illness is never fair, but it did seem particularly unjust that she became so ill, with such a rare form of cancer for which there is currently no cure.

The main objective of the foundation will be to distribute funds to causes that support people with life-limiting illnesses and provide holistic care for both the patient and their families. I have many ideas for fundraising including a launch event in Salisbury Cathedral, where there are a number of Wyndham tombs, sporting events, possibly a ball and any other ideas which will raise significant amounts and reflect my mother's interests. My cousins also get excited about running social events, so watch this space!

The foundation is at its initial stages, but I am very lucky to have the support of my father and brother, who are going to be trustees, and will help to keep me on track if I get too carried away! We plan to distribute our funds to organisations which support people with life-limiting illnesses and also provide support to their families. Unfortunately, my mother's care was lacking and I believe that her experience would have been different if her medical support network had been better. The foundation will support the hospice movement, as hospices make such an enormous difference to families' lives and they receive very limited government funding.

It would be amazing if the Nicola Holliday Foundation could make a difference to even a few people's lives. Life with cancer and other illnesses is so challenging for both the person afflicted and their loved ones. However, if their experience can be alleviated in any small way, it would be very gratifying. And it feels like a very appropriate tribute to my mother who helped so many people and put so much thought into everything. I hope that she will approve.

LUCY HOLLIDAY

JO HAILEY

STRIKING PLACES

Striking Places Photography

I've always had a passion for photography. My first camera was an Olympus Trip when I was 15; when hair products were limited!

Of course back in the olden days it was all 35mm and dark rooms. I was quite ill in my teens with a rare form of cancer and missed a lot of school. Equipped with an A' level in Art I attended Art College. I worked with a photographer in Hatton Garden, London, during the holidays. Photography has always been a passion, although professionally until 2012 I worked as an accountant at the University of Hertfordshire. In my spare time I shot at festivals for free entry and as you'll see on Striking Places website there are a lot of fun festival and dressing up pictures in our collections. Early in 2012 a friend noticed that Google were looking for tech minded photographers for a project they were starting called Google Business Photos. I eagerly applied as I was fascinated that creating Google Street View and high resolution virtual tours was going to be a thing and I could be involved. I bought all the equipment and jumped through the many hoops of certification to become a Google Trusted Photographer.

My biggest achievement so far is, without a shadow of a doubt, shooting Westminster Abbey. It was an honour to work in such a globally recognised historical building. However, it wasn't only the prestige of working with one of the most gorgeous buildings on the planet and gazing at that incredible architecture, but there is another more personal reason for it being uppermost in my list of best bits. My Dad is an official London Tour Guide who specialises in Westminster Abbey. I love a crazy coincidence! In 2015, when the request came through from Westminster Abbey, my Dad had been diagnosed with cancer. The first person I called when I got the request was my Dad. I think it's fair to say that this news perked him right up. Timing and planning for shooting the abbey was a little challenging as it's such a large building with limited clear access. There is only a short period of two and a half hours on Thursday mornings when photography can take place. That's ALL photography too not just little old me. I was competing with big television channels too. Eventually, we booked in the first shoot. There were 7 visits in all. Dad was feeling better towards the date of the first shoot in September 2015 and asked if he could come along. The Westminster Abbey team were fantastic! The response was "we would be delighted to meet your Father". So, Dad got to carry my bags that first morning. :) And I got the fab memento of a panorama of my Dad looking down at the tomb of the unknown warrior.

Of course running your own business doesn't come without its challenges. There have been some massive learning curves. The most notable of these was the realisation that the person I went into business with didn't have the same understanding of business or work ethic as me. I spent 18 months encouraging my business partner to try different ways of working that would more evenly spread the effort between us. Clearly in a 50/50 partnership it was unfair for me to be doing the lion's share of the work. Eventually, I made the decision to call it a day. I guess losing the person in a partnership who makes the business run was a shock to the system. Unreasonable behaviour ensued until, when discussing the situation, a trusted friend offered to step in as mediator. Both my business partner and I agreed and my friend organised a meeting where we thrashed out the heads of terms. As time was not on my side I had to concede to most demands just to bring everything to a close so I could continue running my business and supporting my family. At last I was free from the burden and ready to continue with renewed vigour.

There is no doubt that being your own boss is hard work, much harder work than working for a company or organisation in my experience. There is barely a moment now when I'm not worrying about cash flow, working or thinking about the next shoot, post-production on the next set of images or attending the next networking event. However, what I do, I love meeting new people and understanding their businesses. Creating beautiful imagery to showcase businesses especially with new technologies gives me a real buzz. I also love it when I get a new client as I have the opportunity of showing them what we can do for their business. Overall, living the dream of creating a life where you really can shape your own destiny doing what you love is what makes me get up early and work late. Of course I also have greater flexibility with my time and get to enjoy being around my family when it counts.

Has life changed much now I'm running my own business rather than working for someone else? Yes. Apart from giving a whole new perspective on the world, a few things spring to mind. I'm no longer tied to anyone else's plans. I have all the photographic kit I've ever wanted (well, maybe there are a few other things I could buy....). On a more serious note, the physical and mental health benefits of working for myself cannot be measured. I'm now much more relaxed every day and if I'm having a bad day I can just go and walk the dog. Most of all, I've found myself mixing with people much more like me; business minded.

For anyone considering setting up their own business, it's an incredible experience even with the challenges. If you have a passion for what you do and great product or service, I'd say yes do it! Make sure you are mindful about who you go into business with. It's all very exciting at the beginning and as it starts to grow. However, making a plan and talking about the vision for the future of the business and defining roles and responsibilities will go a huge way towards avoiding my biggest challenge so far.

JO HAILEY
www.strikingplaces.com

NIKKI HOWES
StEPs   STEPS   B**k Banks

St Albans Educational Partnership for Schools (StEPs) C.I.C. was born in 2015 after 15 long years of working for the Local Authority. With a recently vacated spare bedroom turned into StEPs HQ (no time to think about an empty nest), an Amazon Prime membership and my trusty desktop P.C. I set off to change the world...

StEPs was set up to fill an ever increasing gap in Universal and Targeted services for vulnerable people, but especially children and young people, both in St Albans and beyond into Hertfordshire. As the St Albans Schools Partnership Manager, I had spent years building up a superb team of Family Support Workers and Intervention Workers and this team had a huge impact with the families in St Albans, both with parents and with their children. My mission is now, as was then, to improve outcomes for children and young people in our community, no matter what race, gender, social economic status or ethnicity. We pride ourselves on creating innovative and up to date programmes to engage those who would not normally welcome change.

The portfolio has expanded somewhat over the past six months and I am now delivering sessions within the corporate workplace on wellbeing, mindfulness, and managing stress in the workplace. As a traded service, this corporate work allows us to use the profit to part fund some of the sessions we run in schools for children and young people, making it affordable for local schools who have budgets which are getting tighter and tighter. So when you use us, you pay it forward.

Through a varied provision of Parenting courses and workshops, Anger and Self Esteem Interventions for children and young people, Family Support services, Private Coaching and our superb Book Banks© initiative we have reached over 4,000 people in our first two years of trading and the numbers are increasing faster than we can keep pace. Book Banks was born of a passion that I have for reading and my utter conviction that the ability to enjoy reading books of any type can help children succeed. We have wonderful volunteers running fun, interactive sessions across Hertfordshire, mostly within Food Banks and Children's Centres where families can take free books home with them after a fun reading session.

We also work extensively with children and young people with additional needs. We have a range of low cost SEN resources that we sell on Ebay and at SEN fairs. Again, this work allows us to put profit back into delivering front line services.

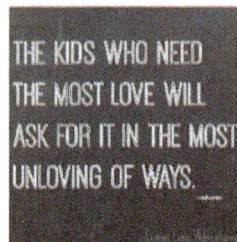

THE KIDS WHO NEED THE MOST LOVE WILL ASK FOR IT IN THE MOST UNLOVING OF WAYS.

Every November and December we work with a local Church and several local schools to run 'Giving Trees'. People are able to buy an extra present for a certain age child and we distribute them through the District in the week before Christmas, mostly through Food Banks, trying to ensure that all children have presents to wake up to on Christmas morning.

Several local businesses also do this for us and donate gifts and money or vouchers and this is just an amazing piece of work that is coordinated by StEPs volunteers across the whole District.

Funding is our biggest monthly agenda item. We are continuously looking for funding so that we can increase capacity and get more programmes out to those that need them, such as Protective Behaviours work. Protective Behaviours is a safety awareness and resilience building programme which helps children and adults to recognise any situation where they feel worried or unsafe, such as feeling stressed, bullied or threatened; and explores practical ways to keep safe. We have been delivering PB's for over 10 years and it has a huge impact on everyone. Recognising, reacting and responding to situations before they develop is key to keeping ourselves and others safe, both physically and emotionally. More and more we are being asked to deliver these sessions in the workplace as well, as the recognition that positive mental wellbeing is as important as physical wellbeing, especially for productivity.

Some of the feedback we have received in the past year includes:

"You have made a huge difference to my family and I just want you to know that."

"Thank you so much for the changes you have made to our family. We are enjoying each other again and have made some big changes with some impact and some tiny changes with huge impact. Who knew it could be better..."

"The two ladies leading the course were superb and extremely knowledgeable - it has made a huge difference to me and my child with special needs."

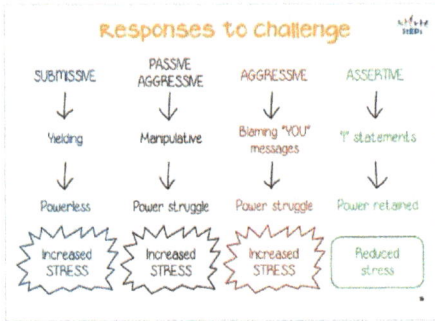

Responses to challenge

SUBMISSIVE	PASSIVE AGGRESSIVE	AGGRESSIVE	ASSERTIVE
↓	↓	↓	↓
Yielding	Manipulative	Blaming "YOU" messages	"I" statements
↓	↓	↓	↓
Powerless	Power struggle	Power struggle	Power retained
Increased STRESS	Increased STRESS	Increased STRESS	Reduced stress

Twitter "Learning how to be a better #parent is one of the most rewarding, and demanding, things I've done. Inspirational work by @StAlbansEPS"

"You have changed the way my family is looking forward to the future. It isn't so desperate now and we are looking forward to the next steps."

"Don't ever let anyone tell you that what you are doing doesn't make a difference and isn't inclusive to everyone, because it is. You have changed the way our family is and I have a new found respect for my wife and what she goes through. You have made us so welcome and part of the group."

NIKKI HOWES
www.stalbanseps.org

CHERYL LUZET
Wagada

Wagada is a digital marketing agency based in St Albans and run by myself and my fantastic team of digital experts. I had worked in the digital arena for many years but saw a gap in the market for a specialist Search Engine Optimisation Agency (SEO) offering high quality services.

At the point that I set up the business SEO was in turmoil: Google had made a lot of changes to improve the quality of search results and ensure that the 'dark art' tactics of the past no longer worked. Many SEO agencies were not equipped to provide this type of service. Clients were frustrated by the lack of transparency and shady sales tactics that some agencies were employing.

Also, many people were turning to web designers for their SEO services, who lacked the specialist skills and day to day hands on experience to get good results.

The aim of Wagada was to change the face of an industry that had a bad reputation, and offer transparent, high quality services to businesses who saw the value of ranking high in the search engines.

When it was time for me to return to work after maternity leave in 2011, I faced the dilemma that many parents face – childcare costs were prohibitive and I found myself in a Catch 22 situation – I couldn't afford not to work, yet I couldn't afford to go to work. I was also concerned that returning to work in London would involve a long commute, taking me away from my children for long periods. I was determined to be around for my children and earn a living. So I decided not to return to my role as a digital consultant in the education sector. Instead I took a leap of faith and, in August 2011, set up my own business, Wagada.

At the time, I was aware of a few local SEO agencies, but felt strongly that there was a real opportunity for Wagada to be a different kind of agency. I had seen first-hand that so many web designers and agencies failed to explain simple concepts and plans to clients, which caused frustration which wasn't necessary. I wanted Wagada to be different.

In those early days, it was a home-based SEO consultancy and I provided high quality SEO services to Hertfordshire SME businesses, but didn't want to stop there. I quickly realised that my clients trusted me and the service I was offering, and they began asking for support with other areas of marketing. I was keen to complement the SEO services that Wagada provided with results-driven, customer-focused digital and traditional marketing services, and my clients soon took me up on these new offerings.

Since then, I have grown the team, and now in 2017 we are a team of 9 in-house staff, and 16 part-time freelancers.

It took me a long time to gain the confidence to build a team. It is a big responsibility and a big step to go from home-based business to leader of people with the overheads of an office. So I worked some very long hours doing the job of two or three people before I built up the confidence to take on an office and employ staff. It's all character building at the end of the day!

As a mum, it was really important for me to be able to work flexibly and this was one of the main motivators for the business. We now offer flexibility to our staff to work as and when they are most efficient and the company has the technology in place to make working from home, or anywhere, easy and effective.

I'm really passionate about the environment we have created at Wagada. Being an employer who can offer flexible working means I get to help other working parents, whilst being a commercially sound, growing and successful business. Flexi working really helps me personally and it helps my business grow. I want great people to work for me and that happens because I offer them a real alternative to the 9-5. Finding high quality experienced staff locally is a challenge, but by offering flexible working we can attract some amazing talent. My team tell me there are tangible benefits to flexible working – they're less stressed; they feel valued; they're more productive; they don't miss out on day-to-day stuff with family; they're motivated to deliver a better quality of work.

It's one of the key reasons I set the business up – I wanted that for myself and for others.

The company has won awards for its flexible working policies: winner of the Flexible Business of the Year Award at the Mum and Working Awards 2016 and Finalist for the Working Mums Champion at the Working Mum Awards, 2016.

What would we say to anyone who is thinking of starting their own business?

Just do it! When I set the company up I had no idea what to expect and no experience in this sort of role. I had worked in a small agency previously and that experience has been invaluable for learning about the different elements of running a business from invoicing to proposals. You need to have faith in yourself when you are running a business – people are buying you and not necessarily the service that you offer. Think about who you are and what you want the business to convey.

Also, get networking! I had never done any form of networking previously and had no idea if it would work for me or not. I surprised myself by enjoying the first experience of it. Networking has been invaluable for the growth of Wagada. It taught me to speak confidently about my business and learn which elements captured people's interest. I also learned a lot about how to run a business from the support network I developed in the networking community in Hertfordshire. Even now, 90% of Wagada's work comes from a connection made at a networking group, whether it is a web designer or marketing consultant looking for SEO support for one of their clients.

You don't have to be an experienced salesperson to develop a successful business. I discovered that many clients were tired of being sold to, and actually a transparent approach where I demonstrated my skills and knowledge was actually the most successful way of gaining new clients and credibility. Finally, don't let yourself get intimidated by strong sales people – this approach can actually be quite off-putting to some people – your aim is to work with those who want to engage with your company and your ideals.

CHERYL LUZET

www.wagada.co.uk

DONNA NICHOL
Chloe James Lifestyle

Looking back I think I always had an entrepreneurial spirit. After school and before university I took a year out to do my own thing. I hired an industrial sewing machine (I can't remember how on earth I managed to do this with no internet!), found a space above a shop in my home town, and set about launching my own clothing range "Wearabouts". This was the 1980s so there was no e-commerce or social media (imagine!) but I did have a steady trade via craft fairs and word of mouth.

Fast forward past university, an exciting career as a fashion buyer travelling the world, predicting trends and placing orders, promotion to Brand Director in charge of a turnover in excess of £40 million, and becoming mum to two lovely kids, and it was time for a change. I had worked for big companies, small companies and growing companies and been very lucky in that, by and large, I had enjoyed all my jobs. The fashion industry is fast-paced, exciting, challenging and fun, full of lots of wonderful hard-working people and a few divas! When I found myself working for the equivalent of Meryl Streep's character in The Devil Wears Prada, I decided enough was enough!

Whilst on maternity leave, first with James and then later with Chloe, I had looked into opening a shop, and so I looked again. As the previous times, there was nothing around that was affordable and in a reasonable location. So I decided to put that plan on hold and launch a wholesale jewellery brand. Why not?! What a learning curve! I headed off to Hong Kong and China on my own to source reliable factories able to do "small" (60-120) quantities, taught myself to design jewellery, created a brand and then learned how to import, sell and distribute it. It wasn't easy, but it was fun and I was doing it for myself. I gradually built up a customer base of hundreds of small independent boutiques and a few bigger clients like Hobbs and Planet. I learned loads but spent a lot of time working on my own and the shop was still my dream. In 2010 I made it happen!

Photograph taken by
Stephanie Belton

Armed with a business plan we started looking for premises. When we stepped into number 12 High Street it was love at first sight. However, it took a long and painful eight months of complicated clauses and expensive solicitor's bills before we finally opened in July 2010. Chloe James Lifestyle was born out of wanting to create something special - somewhere people would love to shop and would come to buy gifts, fashion or items for their home. Somewhere they would be proud to have in St Albans, the sort of place they might have had to travel into London for previously.

Naturally I love the buying! Finding the best products at the right price is what I do best. I have also discovered that I love the selling too - being in the shop chatting to the customers, solving their present/wardrobe/interiors dilemmas, styling the windows, visually merchandising the shop interior, helping women to find their fashion style and feel fabulous! We have so many loyal, returning customers that I'm happy to say they become like friends.

So many great things have happened over the years. We have been on TV twice - once on House Gift with Laurence LLewelyn-Bowen in 2011, and once on The French Collection in 2015. We have taken part in every St Albans Fashion Week and glowed with pride as our outfits graced the 70 metre catwalk in St Albans Abbey. We have become known for our own twice-yearly fashion shows where we raise money for local charities and show around 60 outfits on "real women" models. These events now regularly sell out two weeks in advance (although I still worry about this every time!) We have won lots of awards including "Community Favourite Shop" in 2013 and "Best Specialist Shop" in 2015, and been finalists in many more. Most excitingly of all, we were selected as one of the SmallBiz100 in 2016. This is a national initiative set up to promote small businesses throughout the UK. Each of the 100 businesses had their own day in the run up to Small Business Saturday, when they were promoted all over social media. To top the year off, we were invited to 10 Downing Street for a drinks reception and Chloe James Lifestyle was one of 30 businesses asked to exhibit at this event! We have also recently been selected as one of Theo Paphitis SBS winners.

The best and worst thing about having your own small business is being in charge of everything. It's wonderful to be able to make decisions and get things done without having to jump through too many hoops, but it can be exhausting being in charge 24/7. I think the hardest thing about having a shop in particular, is holding your nerve when sales are slow. We have been open for 7 years now and I still can't help starting to worry if things go a bit quiet. Riding the retail wave is not for the faint-hearted. However, I wouldn't change it! I love the variety of my day/week, I relish tracking down the best products and I really enjoy the interaction with all the different people who walk through the door. One of the most satisfying things for me is hearing the customers chatting to each other about how much they love the shop - it really gives me a warm glow! Oh, and spotting people out and about dressed in Chloe James fashion - I love that too!

Photograph taken by
Ben Askem

My advice to anyone thinking of starting their own business would be "keep at it"! I often hear people say "but how do I know if it's going to work?" Well, you don't, but you really must believe that it is going to work and then you need to work really hard! The difference between success and failure is often just tenacity!

DONNA NICHOL
www.chloejameslifestyle.co.uk

EMMA BUSTAMANTE

Cositas

For as long as I can remember I have always had a passion for colour and form. Growing up, my bedroom floor was covered with sketches of fashion and interior design and I became fascinated with this beautiful creative world. I always dreamed of making it part of my life, but I didn't know how it would come to pass. I forged ahead with a career in retail, starting in retail management, for a well-known womenswear and accessory brand. I learned invaluable skills such as Visual Merchandising, how to maximise the revenue of every inch of the shop floor, lessons that have shaped the way I view product and my customer, lessons that I have carried with me through to present day.

I moved into home interiors and gifts after I had my first two children and needed something to work around my growing family. I found a happy home in a beautiful local shop called Lavendergreen, where I learnt all about the industry and trained as a Chalk Paint teacher.

After ten wonderful years, Lavendergreen closed it's doors, but a new door was about to open for me.

I had three months before Lavendergreen closed, I was faced with a decision; I could find another full time job, or take everything I had learned and pursue a dream of my own.

I am a single parent, with three beautiful children, a dog and a two guinea pigs, I couldn't spend too long dwelling on the panic that started to wash over me, I had to decide on my next step.

Something inside me felt that this might be my moment to start out on my own. It felt as though my life was about to change forever. This was the catalyst I needed to make a change, to take a leap of faith and just go for it!

And so that's what I did! With no capital of my own, I knew that my first step was to secure a business loan. But where to start!? I spent a tough couple of months writing, amending, rewriting, submitting and resubmitting business plan after business plan, with the help of some great people around me.

I was working under pressure with the knowledge that I only had this three month window to turn my dream into a tangible reality before Lavendergreen closed its doors for the last time and my final paycheque was issued. It forced me to be more focused and organised than ever before. I found that I was more determined and braver than I ever thought I could be.

The initial challenge of securing the Business Start-Up loan almost had me falling at the first hurdle. The business plan and cash flows were so in depth, they also required me to proceed so far down the line with a securing a premises, that I needed the help of a solicitor and an accountant before I had even secured the finances. At the time it felt like a huge gamble to start paying out such expenses that I didn't really have. I didn't even know if my loan would be approved, but in order to just try, I had no other choice but to bet on myself and keep moving forwards. Luckily, I've been wholly invested in this project from the get-go and truly believed in my vision, determined to make it work one way or another.

My vision was a store in the heart of St Albans called Cositas. Cositas means 'Little Things,' in Spanish, a nod to my Chilean heritage. My vision was to bring together a fusion of vintage and contemporary interiors and offers customers the opportunity to attend creative workshops and courses to create something beautiful for themselves. I wanted to give customers the opportunity to mix around with a range of styles, as well as learning and developing their own skills about how to update their homes in stylish ways.

As soon as I saw my shop on Holywell Hill I fell in love. When I walked around for the first time I knew it was the "one". I used my Start Up capital to secure my rent, set up the retail software/ infrastructure, and kit out the shop with stock. I made decisions about what I wanted Cositas to be, who I wanted it to be for- each and every piece has been lovingly chosen with my customer in mind. Everyday was new, every challenge was fresh, but I approached every moment with joy and excitement. I'm learning more now, than ever before.

I've been lucky enough to be working alongside some incredibly talented folk, in the form of accountants, web designers, printers, independent suppliers and friends and family who have offered me their invaluable time, help and advice and for that, I'll be forever grateful. Supportive networks such as this St Albans Business Group has given me

comfort and overwhelming support, which has helped keep me confident and motivated.

I have just had my two teenage daughters conduct work experience with me. To have them in our shop, working together, brought me so much pride- they, and my son, are my motivation for everything. Everything I do, I do to provide and create a better life for me and my children and I can't believe that I am in a position where I can do this for us every day.

Every time someone compliments the shop, it brings me such joy and the fact that men seem to love my shop as much as the women do, is one of my greatest achievements so far! I love that shop seems to have universal appeal for both sexes and that such a varied audience are inspired by the pieces that we have curated in store.

I have such high hopes and plans for Cositas. We are launching Cositas Creative Workshops in September 2017 a full, busy, packed calendar of incredible creative workshops, from furniture making to abstract art and everything in between. I'm passionate about creating a hub for creative people, a place where people can share ideas, learn skills, and improve their wellbeing by taking time out to make something beautiful for their homes. Our online store will be as vibrant as our street store soon and I can't wait to take on this digital world too. There's so much more to come. Being ambitious has made me even more ambitious - I get new ideas every day and I'm so excited to bring them all to life.

My advice to anyone who is thinking about starting their own business is to be brave. You are stronger, more resilient and more determined than you know. By pushing yourself, you'll only scratch the surface of how far you can go. Surround yourselves with people you trust who can help you.

This time last year, I was working in an Interiors store in St Albans and now I'm running a shop of my very own. Every evening as I lock up, I look around at the pieces that I have selected, the furniture that me and my staff have carefully placed, the name on our door that I thought of at home with my children and I just can't believe that I did it. If I can do it, you can do it and I hope you take the leap and do.

EMMA BUSTAMANTE
www.cositas.co.uk

SALLY SHEPHERD

EVE & ADAM Boutique Spa   **Eve & Adam Boutique Spa**

12 Catherine Street, St Albans, AL3 5BX

INSPIRATION

Coming from a background of entrepreneurs I suppose it seemed inevitable that one day I would work for myself. My paternal Grandfather, son of a butcher, was working as a builders Clerk in Tottenham at the time of the expansion of the railways. He speculated Watford Junction was the next hot spot outside of London, and saw an opportunity for housing. Raising money, he bought a few plots of land and built streets of houses that are now Victorian terraces. He then went on to be the Mayor of Watford 1925-26. Yes …a generation skipped as my grandfather sired my dad at the age of 70!

My maternal Grandfather was one of 11 children brought up in Harlesden. He started with a barrow in the original Covent Garden, selling fruit and veg. After hard graft he bought his first shop, then another and created a highly regarded 'fruiterers' business at the time of the second world war. Word is, he did well out of the black market, and then moved his family out to leafy Hertfordshire, where he and my grandmother seemingly enjoyed a lavish lifestyle of glamorous parties and horseracing – that is what I can recall!

BACKGROUND

I grew up on a farm with no mobiles and restricted Television whilst my siblings hared around on bikes in the fields making camps etc, as many of my generation, I was usually found painting stones, making perfume out of rose petals or bagging up manure in old seed bags. All of these I sold at the end of the drive each weekend! Even at the age of 7 I loved the feel of money in my hands.

Art was my thing, and I went on to do Art A level and a foundation course. I avoided Uni as I was desperate to get out into the world of commerce and snared a job in a local interior Design business, where I furnished show houses. I moved into Graphic design and eventually marketing.

SO, how did I end up working for myself and, in the beauty business?

Between ages 19-23, I experienced 4 successive and frightening life changing events that resulted in a decision to take a sabbatical, and travel on my own. Against everyone's wishes, I backpacked, hiked and camped meeting some crazy but inspirational people. Probably becoming a bit of a hippy, I learned to meditate which enabled me to sleep for the first time in years. This opened my eyes to a more holistic approach to life, realizing how linked the body and mind were. Because of this, on my return home I trained in Anatomy & Physiology whilst continuing in marketing at a Branding Agency. Then devastatingly - my mum died.

That was the cathartic moment when I knew that I needed to take absolute control of my life and work for myself. Now life was too short to waste. I didn't want the shackles of 28 days holiday a year and I yearned a flexible day ungoverned by a timesheet. I needed freedom. I also very much wanted to make a difference to people's wellbeing and happiness, rather than just deliver a corporate brochure, for example, on time. So, I decided to get fully trained in the Beauty industry whilst gaining experience in a health club.

THE BUSINESS

I founded Eve & Adam Spa in 2003 along with a business partner. We put together our business plan, formulated our business model and found the premises. I then discovered I was pregnant and had the option to put the business on hold. I elected to continue and 7 Weeks before we opened, I gave birth to my daughter.

The first 3 years of hers and the business lives, were beyond crazy. As a single parent with no local family, it was some days, seemingly impossible. But, I was fortunate I had supportive friends and an excellent team which enabled me much more flexible working.

The decision to open the business, and not put it on the back burner, was for me the right one. Knowing now what it is like to have a young child and run a business, in reality I don't think I would ever have started it. But it is a 'lifestyle business 'that suits my needs and the way I wanted to live my life.

Now 14 years on we have a successful, innovative and established salon and created a good business model to enable expansion.

MOTIVATION

My motivation is driven by:

a) Knowing our business makes a real difference to our client's wellbeing. There is real-time trackable and visible evidence!

b) Knowing I can be ultimately independent.

c) Seeing my team evolve in their profession.

d) Being a role model to my daughter as a working mother.

TIPS AND ADVICE

a) Embrace and encourage competition. It keeps you on your toes and you can learn from and help each other out (My grandfather's tip).

b) Never underestimate what you need to live on. Overestimate your personal monetary needs - this is good Housekeeping. It is all very well having a flexible lifestyle but if you can't afford to live, it could be miserable.

c) 'If at first you don't succeed...' If something doesn't work out look for a different way. There are many twists and turns that can block your path. But, these are just stumbling ones. You will have learned something from each one. Pick yourself up and look again, as there is always a way. But you have got to really want it.

d) Do not be a control freak and think you can, or need to wear every 'hat'. Don't be afraid to delegate. Delegation will unclip your wings and be amazed at how much more you are capable of!

e) Running your own business - If it was easy then everyone would do it. The lows may seem greater but the highs will far outweigh them.

SALLY SHEPHERD

www.eve-and-adam.com

CHRISTO TOFALLI

Ye Olde Fighting Cocks (reputed to be Britain's oldest pub)

I was never supposed to own a pub, it simply wasn't the plan. My wife Sarah and two young boys Alex, 8 and Thomas, 5 were in the final stages of moving to Australia, sadly at the same time my brother lost his fight with cancer and we decided to stay in St Albans close to our family.

When I spoke to friends about buying the pub, they thought I was mad, and to be honest they were right. All they could see was that we were putting everything into a failing, dirty, and turns out, completely broken pub. They were right about that too. What they couldn't see was a pub St Albans would be proud of and one day a business that would pay back our financial investment with profit. Although after five years and one hundred days, the financial investment is nowhere near being repaid, we are feeling bullish and can see the beginning of a new existence of making a profit; very small but still a profit.

Our biggest struggles have often become our biggest successes. The first one cost us our house, a quite innocent mistake to make but make sure if you have a business partner, your agendas are the same. With the best will in the world, if you are looking at a business from two different angles, it doesn't work. Both wanting a good pub but there are good pubs and there are pubs

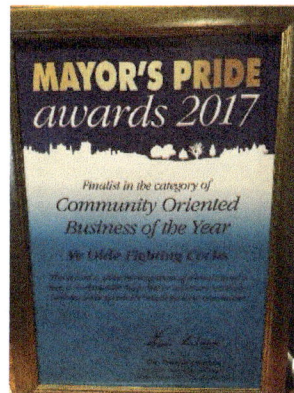

that are good. The success bit of this is that we are now through this and luckily it was all resolved amicably, after all, what's a house between friends. We now own all the lease and have managed to stay in business all by ourselves. The cost to us was everything, all of it. We managed to buy the lease, pay all the extortionate and 90% unnecessary fees that go with buying a business (don't get me started on moaning about fees, that is a whole other book and it would also be x rated). The only money we owned was the £1,000.00 we had in the tills for float. The next bill would have to have been paid out of the till, there was no more money, anywhere. Thankfully, they have all been paid since then.

Another struggle was on the day we moved in finding out all the equipment, electrics, plumbing, kitchen, cellar and bar was working but all on life support. We saw it working when we visited but didn't look with eyes wide open. I was so intent on getting the pub, I looked passed all the things that I would notice now. If I was in the position to look at another business or pub, no matter how enthusiastic I may feel, I will look without emotion when inspecting anything, especially myself. Having said that, anyone that knows me would say I fail at this on an hourly basis but I like to think I manage it on important issues.

I am still having the time of my life, so much has happened, our achievements have been massive starting with being solvent! Yay! To winning awards and recognition from the ones that do the recognising. From CAMRA (Silver medal winner 2017) to Cask Marque measuring beer quality, a Mayor's Pride nomination for Business in the Community and to two of my favourites. The first was our first five-star Environmental Health report which for a very small facility serving lots of food, our hygiene was good but we always lost points in the age of the kitchen in general. We didn't only inherit an old nearly not working kitchen, but I would call a lack of love in anything that happened for the previous five decades. To get a five-star rating, you have to be working well on all levels, from your everyday practice to the equipment we invested in and most importantly the time we gave the staff. The entire team needs to be working with the same agenda in mind, it didn't matter what their individual motivations were, everyone from top to bottom back to front and round the entire place pulled in the same direction. The biggest achievements of the pub are the ones I see in my team winning their own battles, like taking a young 16-year-old washer upper, he doesn't mind me saying he was a slow (I have used other words) washer upper, Leon has been at the pub for around five years now. He has stuck by his post no matter what he was asked to do, when I was chef he held me up when I needed it, he never gave up. Ever. He is now a sous chef in an award-winning pub with a career and being paid properly for it too. I am so proud of him, as I am of many others.

So, my food and drink career started in April 2012 at YOFC (Ye Olde Fighting Cocks). I now have experience in every part of the pub. From kitchen porter and eventually through to a very tough but rewarding head chef for eight months. I have also worked through collecting glasses to waiting tables to barman and general front of house and of course landlord. Learning how to manage a cellar that Cask Marque approved of was one another job. Along with weeding to building and renovating the garden and very recently the inside of the pub. My job roll now after just over five years is mainly front of house, running the business and relieving pressure wherever it's needed. The first place is usually washing up in the kitchen or washing glasses for the front of house. All the other operational management bases are covered these days, that's simply where I seem to fit in best when we are busy. The other way of putting it is I always get in the way.

In the last year or two, I have been able to focus on working within our community on various projects, all of them worthy and all of them affecting our community. Our core values start at the pub and spread out from there. The first major local project we undertook was to clear a large area of land to create more space for Earthworks, which is an organic farm run by people with learning disabilities, who are now friends. When they are able, we still buy as much produce from them as possible as well as still being our number one charity. We buy as much as possible locally and always prefer like-minded independent businesses from our fruit and veg supplier to a new local brewery to brew our own beer using our staff.

All of our local independent suppliers have grown with us, from the man that bakes our bread, and brioche buns to the fruit and veg to cheese to Earthworks and beyond. To carry on paying our suppliers weekly and being a good company to deal with is not only important to us but to our suppliers. Investing within our own staff to train them to deliver the best they can, our job at the oldest pub is important on so many levels being such an historic building.

Before we moved in, tourists were happy to walk in the pub but were disappointed by the time they walked out. The case is very different now we are very proud to say. All of this is driving tourism which helps every business in the area.

If you visit now, your timing will be perfect as the pub is the best it has ever been over the last thousand or so years. Hurry up!

If I was to say anything to someone wanting to start a business I will quote something that was written to me by someone I respect and who our head chef trained under around 15 years ago, Ruth Hurren formally of the amazingly delicious Darcy's in St Albans. "Keep tough and fair, don't lose sight of what you are about and want". I was on my backside when Ruth wrote this, it kept me going. I still read it and it means as much to me now as it did then, I have thanked Ruth in person recently and was lucky enough to tell the great Lady it's like having an ace in my deck.

Current holders of Best Pub in the St Albans Food and Drink Awards. Nominated for the recent Mayor's Pride Awards for Business within the Community. Current Silver Medal Winners of South Hertfordshire Pub of the year for CAMRA for the first time in our history. Cask Marque accreditation. Maximum Food and Hygiene rating of five stars. Nominated for Best Pub in Hertfordshire but no winner's award... Yet!

CHRISTO TOFALLI
www.yeoldefightingcocks.co.uk

KIM BRADFORD

Sphere HR

Unlike many HR professionals, I fell into this field. Or rather, I fell into recruitment, which then led later into a move to HR. Originally, I worked in retail as a visual merchandiser, then spent some time in sales (photocopiers, if you must know) before being hired by a London recruitment company. I went from a lonely and thankless job flogging office equipment to office managers, to recruiting and placing those same office managers; it was an induction into a 'work family' and a way of life that I was not expecting, but it formed the basis for a fascinating career.

Fast forward almost 20 years, across 3 continents and many different employers later, and I can look back on an interesting professional interim career as an HR Consultant. It's been fun, challenging, entertaining, frustrating, and educational. I've worked in a broad cross-sector of industries, from airline to shipping, to warehousing and supply chain; from bookmakers to lottery managers, charities to start-ups, banks to research organisations, and from IT to manufacturing. Across these industries I experienced HR in all its glorious forms, good and bad.

I concluded to myself that managing human resources as a function and a practice, whilst essentially a core and basic element of any business, is never done in the same way in any two companies; it's not rocket science, but it is a science, and often an art as well. It dawned on me that bigger businesses were often struggling with a function that hadn't grown up at the same speed or with the same embrace from senior leaders within the company that other essential functions had, such as Finance or IT.

That was the source of puzzlement for me, but as I began working with smaller businesses I began to see why – very few start-ups and micro or small businesses I came across had any kind of HR input or focus from the beginning. Not until they grew to the size where the MD and senior partners couldn't deal with the day to day management of 'people stuff' did they start thinking about HR, and then it was a practical function, such as managing payroll, or looking after basics like policies, contracts, and everyday employee issues: niggles between staff, queries about flexible working and family leave, holiday and absence management. HR never formed an active and integral part of business strategy from the word 'go'.

My epiphany came when working with a small IT firm – the owner, an independent IT contractor, grew to have more work than he could manage, so took on a couple of employees to help. Suddenly he found he was spending his time managing the employees, and had no time to spend on either the work he had won, or on prospective clients. Caught in a catch 22, disheartened that his staff didn't share his vision for the business, and unable to maintain its growth, he stopped paying himself, and finally realised he needed to close his business and let his staff go.

In supporting him through this bruising experience I realised that small businesses were the ones who MOST needed the advice and support I could offer; not as a permanent employee, but as an ad hoc consultant, someone who could guide and advise them at the beginning and early stages of their journey. At the same time, I read a report on the UK business makeup and learned (to my shock) that 99.9% of UK companies are designated as SMEs (small and medium businesses), employing 60% of all the UK's workers. That's 5.2 million businesses, and 15.7 million workers, that are keeping the UK economy running! Picture my jaw dropping.

Ok, many are micro businesses, meaning they employ less than 9 people, but when considering the failure rate for small businesses (40% fold in the first 5 years) I couldn't shake the thought that this was where I should be. And so, I turned my back on the bigger companies with the exciting HR projects, and decided to focus instead on working with smaller, local companies, micro businesses and SMEs.

My biggest struggle, in the early stages of my venture to be an HR consultant to small and micro businesses, was learning to change my corporate HR language, and instead speak the language of my target market. I learnt this through trying to devise SEO for my website: a small business owner in need of help with staff at loggerheads with each other is less likely to google "I need an HR consultant to help with my employee relations" and far more likely to instead reach out to their networks for some help with staff issues.

I need to be in front of people to start the right conversations about the services I can provide, so I've learned the value and power of local business networking, which has in turn taught me a great deal in a short space of time about what drives and motivates small business owners – I've discovered a massive complex business world operating all around me that I was never even aware of before, and that is both a powerful and humbling discovery.   It's also, strangely, what keeps me motivated and on my chosen path.

It's a lonely thing, being a business owner or entrepreneur – knowing when to hire new people to join the team is a big move, and once you move from 'sole trader' to 'employer' life will fundamentally change.   Not everyone is prepared for it, the journey can be rough during the early stages of growth; employing people isn't easy, though we all take it completely for granted. What is needed (in spades!) is self-belief, good advice from specialists to get your business, accounts, and social media set up, and understanding from family and friends.

My advice is to ensure you have a clear idea of what you want to do, how you will make a start, and what your small everyday goals will be as well as your bigger milestones.   Having some money in the bank or an income of some description keeps the stress of looming bills and mortgage payments from crushing your spirit, or your family from worrying about your finances. You also need to understand how to put some structure into your days – you will not necessarily be in a typical 9-5 office environment, and I for one fought a feeling of guilt for 'faffing about on the internet' for days on end until I gave myself a firm talking to about it being part and parcel of my new 'job'.

KIM BRADFORD
www.spherehr.co.uk

DAVID JENKINS

PQA Hemel Hempstead & St Albans
Brilliant Theatre Arts
Brilliant Management

David Jenkins, FRSA: the accidental business man.

Being brought up in a small village in South Wales, there aren't any overwhelming success stories unless it is celebrating the achievement of our local darts team. One thing I always had was an understated work ethic which I, having looked closely at my family, probably inherited from my Nan.

Growing up and getting an education was a challenge, especially with our school under achieving at most things. But, with every success story there always should be a back story. I will keep mine brief.

Being brought up by a single parent of two, me being the oldest, there are a few things that are apparent. If you want something that badly, it is probably not going to happen. I wanted a lot! New clothes, trips with the school, a video and a simple trip to Disneyland. Not much to ask, right? I mean, there was this money tree my mum kept talking about.

So, if I wanted food I was better off cooking it for myself, if I wanted nice things I was better off not thinking about it. This, at the time, was, in my eyes, bad parenting! In fact border line neglect. 'Wise words' were being repeated constantly by my mother "If you want something that bad you must work for it!".

When I was twelve I managed to secure myself a milk round which started at 3am. I also bagged a paper round off a friend who "couldn't be bothered" starting at 6.30am. I did this for three years on and off apart from on Sundays, getting up at 3am, getting dropped off at the newsagents at 6.30am until 7.45am, then straight home to shower and catch the 8.30am bus to school - all for £30 per week.

Fast forward through my average (not terrible) exam results, a misguided attempt at college, and I fell into theatre. The whole journey of that I will keep for my memoirs, but it was home. I spent the next few years working hard for a few different companies backstage and onstage. After years of turning up on time, working hard, first one in and last one out, I got asked to be stage manager. Nineteen years old with 'responsibility' I was shoe horned in, given a team of people ALL older than me and was told 'not to mess it up'.

Let's say it started smoothly, I could do all the work with my amazing team willing to watch. Dictating was never my strong point. The shows got bigger, my team got stronger and I had a lot on my plate. Being twenty-two years old with the entire world on your shoulders was never my intention, so, I decided to focus on my deep passion; performing! 'Stepping into the dark side' as they say in the business. Fast forward a few years, some professional training, a life changing operation and I was a trained actor.

Now what?

The best advice I was ever given was by a horse whisperer. Read the Celestine Prophecies, which I urge you all to read. It has advice tips on getting that thing you want. You see with the power of the universe apparently the more you ask and believe, the more you attract. So, with that advice I sent out ten applications each day for a month, thinking the laws of probability will bring something my way.

It did, I was offered a placement working for Merlin entertainment at The Alton Towers Resort. They paid me well, I was surrounded by a talented team and I got to showcase my endless energy. It was there where my entrepreneur side started to show. I was asked if I ever did kids parties, to which I replied; "YES, of course I do, my company specialises in them."

My company?... I best get a company then. I bought a company name, that was easy, registered a domain name, easy! My good friend designed me a logo, I had some t-shirts printed and my new company was born. Fast forward two years, the party business was doing extremely well with more parties coming in than I could handle and disco requests galore. I finally got approached by the local rag to offer me the Stoke-on-Trent's entrepreneur of the year award. WOW!

Then my thoughts of being stuck in Stafford for the rest of my life and not following my dream (or practicing what I had trained for) ate away at me. So, I tipped my cap and took a risk by moving to London to be an Actor. Using my laws of the universe, please see above for the technique, I finally received interest from a few agents. Lots of "No!", but that was okay, I have been told no for years - it just made me want it more. I finally went to an office in Charing Cross Road and signed with a huge agent. Life was good.

Fast forward a year or two and I was doing more leafleting than acting, but I was in London. My agent didn't work for me so I had a big decision, was I to put my career in someone else's hands again or give it to the best salesman I know.... Me! So, I called up and enquired how to register as an agency and they said, "Do you have an agency and do you represent five actors or more?" "Of course" I replied, "I will send details over".

A company? I best get a company then. Luckily, I already had a name, and I knew a load of actors that would have killed for someone to represent them, and the fact that it was me, let's just say they bit my arm off.

Fast forward a few years and some real considerable success stories, I started to lose focus on my own happiness. So, I took a year out to spend some time travelling the world, entertaining again only to come back with the age-old question... What now?

After randomly landing a big advert/marketing contract with a huge supermarkets mobile phone campaign, I was then approached by a company who offered me my own Performing Arts Academy.

A new challenge, I admit, and one that I might have been more interested in, in the future, but you do not get an offer like this every day and you know me, I like a challenge.

I took on a relatively small academy and promised them grandiose things. Now fast forward four years and I have three full academies spread over two large areas, I also own my very own youth group company producing shows around the UK as well as a management agency with thirty plus professional actors on our books. I have eleven staff, seven of which are full time.

Now, I am not going to sit here and convince you to become a businessperson and impress you with figures and returns, but I will say to all those who read this and are wondering if they should go for it, if you really believe there is a place for what you are offering then yes! My advice is this: business is 20% product and 70% the person/people.

I would not have gotten to this point without offering a little bit of myself to everyone, sometimes working for less than nothing with the hope that would be remembered, and with a sense of hard work and a bit of sheer persistence.

I wake up every day striving to be the best and offer the best. My age-old saying is you should not be here to take over, but to really take part. My business ethos is to work hard and over time you will get results. I am only thirty-two at the time of writing this. Sixteen years in the making and I am still growing, plus, I still haven't finished.

My final words are this; do something you believe in but more importantly, believe in yourself!

DAVID JENKINS

www.pqacademy.com
www.brillianttheatrearts.co.uk
www.brilliant-management.co.uk

CATHERINE BATOUR

Make Up Beauty Fashion

My name is Catherine Batour, Make Up Artist and Beautician. I have a passion for makeup, beauty and fashion inspired by my stylish mother and initiated further when I was given a beautiful makeup pallet from her friend, showcasing an array of fabulous eyeshadow colours in my teenage years. Whilst at school, I started to think about my career and it was my mother who saw an advertisement looking for school leavers to join luxury department store Harrods and I successfully joined their management-training scheme. This allowed me to gain valuable work experience whilst studying Business Finance, Marketing and Law at Hammersmith and West London College. In my first week at Harrods, I was given a talk on 'how to portray a polished image' from world renowned cosmetic house Estée Lauder who advised on the importance of wearing at least nine different makeup products, as well as having regular manicures and pedicures! This gave me an insight into first impressions and 'image', which I found fascinating and to this day, I still like to have matching polish on fingers and toes and I would rather go without polish than have chipped nails! My glamorous aunt gave me my first Chanel Red Lipstick when I was 17, which I still wear and use today!

I spent three years training and moving through various departments in Harrods from shop floor Sales, Fashion Buying, Press, Marketing and Human Resources. I held a number of positions during my seventeen years, some of which include

Fashion and Beauty Assistant Press Officer, Fashion Co-Ordinator, Fashion Buyers Clerk, Personal Shopper, PA to the Managing Director ending with my last position being 'Business Development Manager of CRM and Marketing Manager of 'Harrods By Appointment' which involved me launching Harrods first loyalty rewards programme and a By Invitation only exclusive Personal Shopping service. In 2006, I left Harrods to join another prestigious brand I had always wanted to work for - American Express. I started as 'Membership Rewards Executive' and was later promoted to 'Head of Lifestyle Business Development' for their exclusive and the ultimate in the world of charge cards - Centurion and Platinum cards, where I was part of the launch of the exclusive sought after Titanium card.

After six years at American Express I took a few years off whilst I had two lovely children, but realised I didn't want to go back into London and I had the opportunity to use this time to learn a new skill. I went back to college to study Beauty Therapy for 12 months, and when I qualified I went on to study Fashion and Photographic Make Up. I totally underestimated the syllabus and workload and how much I needed to understand about science, chemistry, artistry, psychology whilst interpreting trends in fashion and make up. I was working late every night and weekends just to keep up with the coursework and information that I needed to take on board. Whilst this was both exciting and challenging, especially with two children under two, I still kept in contact with American Express, as I wasn't sure if I was returning back or not! Quickly, I realised that I had found a new calling – which allowed me to look after my children and work. So, after qualifying I took a leap

of faith and launched my own business – which I thought of as a hobby (originally called 'Beauté bybatour'). I met so many like-minded people who encouraged and supported me. I continued training to refine my skills with Shellac Education, allowing me to offer manicures and pedicures using Shellac and Vinylux nail polish system and also joined Organic British skincare company 'Neal's Yard' as an Independent Consultant and business group - 'St. Albans Businesses'.

The biggest challenge was retraining whilst having very young children, and getting known within the beauty industry. I have grown my client base through regular clients who have recommended me to their friends and more recently through working on other local initiatives. I could not have changed my career without the support of my husband who has been incredible throughout my journey and often cancelled social engagements to allow me to retrain and develop - nothing was too much trouble and he held the fort and looked after our angels (then 9 months and a 2 years) whilst I attended the necessary training - he also has a full time job often working until the early hours and at weekends! I am incredibly appreciative and lucky to be able to have a second career opportunity at this stage of my life.

My biggest achievement was being asked to join the charity 'Look Good Feel Better'. I am able to use my skills and passion for skincare and make up to help people who have had their lives disrupted by cancer.

The most satisfying part of my business is seeing the reaction of people after they have had a makeup session. Many have lost their confidence in makeup and are surprised to see the results! My life has changed for the better and I feel I have taken control of my time and I am able to have a career around my family. I feel less pressured than before as I control my workload, unlike my time in the corporate world.

My motivation comes from meeting new people, client satisfaction and keeping up to date with industry trends - I am now able to adapt parts of my old career into my own business, which is constantly evolving. I do feel that without the years of training I had, I would not have felt confident enough to start my own business. My inspiration comes from my immediate and extended family who have a positive outlook on life and a strong work ethic, who throughout their lives have adapted to challenges and changes thrown their way. My Gran always told me that my priority is my family and to have faith in all that I do and my father one said 'Life is not a re-run just enjoy'. And I really am!

I would like to give a message to anyone looking at starting a business; just take that leap of faith as I did and you will make it work - do something you are passionate about and try not to worry about other people's opinions. A lot of thought went into giving up my last job to work for myself as I had worked so hard toward this dream job and the opportunities and life experiences it brought. I wouldn't have been able to do that without my years of experience in the luxury market. It hasn't been smooth sailing – I was fearful of being criticised and failing and not being in my comfort zone. However, my family and friends have been wonderfully supportive - and those fears have now gone. Always remember, nothing ventured is nothing gained and you can always try something else if things are not going as planned.

I do miss the hustle and bustle of working in London, which has given me incredible experiences and lifelong friends from all over the world - I don't however miss the daily commute and train delays!

I'm so excited for what the future holds and have met some wonderful people through starting my business - many of whom have been in a similar situation and together we are looking at an exciting time ahead of us.

I'm currently working with some amazing fashion boutiques and talented photographers on some fabulous events and projects and I am so pleased to be able to share my story with you.

CATHERINE BATOUR
www.catherinebatour.com

NEIL BARRAS-SMITH

WILL TRUST & PROTECT Will Trust & Protect Ltd

The best way to predict your future is to create it.

I'm sure we've all had dreams of being rich, and I was no different to anyone else. I fully believed I would make it, and that success was inevitable. Being creative and intuitive, I would imagine different business ideas, and how they would bring me the wealth of my dreams, but idea after idea came and went without any ever becoming fully formed, I was a viewer not a doer! Then in my 30's it hit me; how much money is enough money?

Some of my friends were earning 6 figure salaries – not the wealth of my dreams, but not far off it, yet they didn't seem any happier than me. I had a wonderful family, a lovely house, two nice cars on the drive, two holidays a year, and even enough disposable income for the odd slap up meal at our favourite restaurant, and I seemed more content than any of my peers. I had made my mind up; This was all I needed, and nothing more.

After doing numerous jobs over the years from sales rep, to engineer, I found myself working for the Police force, and after 10 years of supporting the boys and girls in blue, I eventually arrived at the point where I wasn't experiencing any job satisfaction. The routine of it all was chipping away at my personality as I didn't feel I was making a difference. I had lost all interest in what I was doing for a living, and I decided I needed a challenge. If only I could find something new to focus us on; something to get out of bed in the morning for, and something I was doing for me.

I no longer wanted to be that person that looked out from my office window, in envy at those who felt constantly energised by the exciting difference every day brings when running your own business. I took the daunting step of a career break, albeit with the safety net that I could return to a job with the Police force within a year.

The purchase of my first buy-to-let property gave me a small income each month, and that helped supplement my outgoings.

As I embarked on my first business venture, a few things were very important to me: It didn't matter if I earnt £50k or £500k, the fact I was working for myself, making my own decisions, and not making someone else rich whilst I just received a standard salary was key.

I needed to do a job that gave me satisfaction; too many of my previous roles turned quickly into mind-numbing routine, and I lost motivation.

I wanted to help people by providing a service that was necessary, but that gave me pride in knowing I helped make peoples' lives better in some way.

Throughout my career to that point I had never felt that I was making a difference despite my best efforts to go the extra mile.

One year before I took my career break, my beloved grandmother, who had been suffering from dementia, was sadly deteriorating, and we had no other option but to move her to a care home. After dealing hands on with the entire process, including the sale of her home, I decided I would like to offer my help to others unfortunate enough to have to go through this momentous change in their lives. This life experience moulded every aspect of my intentions to work for myself, and too make a difference. So, I created my company, Care Relocation, and started out on a new journey, all on my own. Like any start-up business, you don't need me to tell you; it's hard! The initial process was complex, and responsible for several sleepless nights. Creating Business plans, obtaining funding, dealing with Companies' house, accountants, insurances, marketing, websites, literature; the list seems to be endless. Each element can take up most, if not all your time if you let it. Trying to understand business processes, that you have never had to face up to before whilst trying to be all things to all people, can become overwhelming. If running your own business gives you one thing in abundance, it is countless opportunities to walk away!

I was fortunate enough to have a good friend within a care home group who put me in contact with the right person. Following a meeting with them, I came away with a real belief in what I, and my company stood for. That invaluable contact gave me an initial break by allowing me to put my brochures into 27 of their care homes, and allowed me to send out my brochure with every enquiry pack they dispatched to potential clients. It was a surprise, and a relief to find that an expert within the industry found real value in the service I wanted to provide. This was the affirmation I needed to spur me on. All seemed to be going well, but challenging times were around the corner.

After a year of concentrating wholly on my exciting new venture, I had to reluctantly put things on hold due to difficulties in my personal life. The change in direction I took may not have added strain on my relationship with my family, but all the same, I decided I had no option but to put my entrepreneurial dreams on hold to concentrate on being a Dad. As soon as things looked settled in my personal life, normality was quickly restored, and I decided to return to my business. I'd quickly built several valuable contacts in what I regarded as round 1 of my new career, so I put ego to one side, and went looking for support. On day one of round 2, I approached a contact, John, who had built his own successful estate planning business in Shefford, Beds. He had some spare desk space which he kindly agreed to rent to me as a base for my company, and it wasn't long before John approached me with a request to work with him on the expansion of his business. John was in the process of opening a new branch in Enfield, North London. Within 2 weeks of working on this project it became quite apparent that John needed me more than we both anticipated. I was offered a very attractive salary, but I sat back, considered how I had got to this point and boldly asked for a share in the business. This was key to me, and one of the core reasons I changed career direction in the first place. I didn't want to just create something for someone else; I wanted to create something for both of us. My dream was still to run my very own business, something I had worked so hard to this point for, but I looked on this opportunity as more than just a stepping stone. With the additional skills I would learn, this opportunity would help me to provide a more complete service to my clients. So, after 6 months of helping expand Will, Trust and Protect, and spending many hours training, we are now about to open our third branch of Will, Trust and Protect in sunny St Albans.

As part of my personal development to be the best businessman I can be, I have thrown myself into the Estate Planning industry whole-heartedly, and after gaining a qualification as a Will Writer through the Society of Will Writers, I am also well on my way to becoming an Independent Mortgage Advisor after passing the first CeMap exams. The desire to help protect peoples' futures is what drives us at WTAP. I may have ended up in a slightly different place to where I intended, but there is an undeniable synergy with my original business Idea to provide the much-needed support to those moving into care, and this service will soon become part of our exciting expansion. Life takes unexpected, sometimes exciting turns, but you must move forward in some way to get to those turns. There will always be ups and downs as an entrepreneur, but if you believe in what you want to do, and do it with passion, and desire to help your customers, then chances are you will be successful.

NEIL BARRAS-SMITH
www.willtrustandprotect.co.uk

SUE WYBROW
Popdance

I never wanted a career, or to run my own business. I simply wanted to earn money, go home and live my life.

I didn't have big ambitions, but I knew I always wanted my independence. And my mum even says to me now how independent I was as a kid and that I never wanted to miss out on anything - always had ants in my pants.

So, I started a paper round at aged 13, which I then added to by working in a bakers shop every Saturday, and then at one point I had three jobs, which included working in a bank when I was 16!

I wasn't a real fan of school, I loved writing but didn't love school life - I wanted to make money and be able to do what I wanted to do.

So, even before I finished school, I applied for jobs in a bank - a good solid foundation for a career, said my parents, and my sister was working for Barclays at the time, so I applied for a few jobs and got offered Bank of England, Lloyds and Midland. Bank of England was far too stuffy for me at the time and Midland were paying £3 more a year! So I went for them! Based in the area office in Baker Street, London, I thought I'd hit the big time - and I had! Working with other 16 year olds, as well as the more experienced staff, I enjoyed my 2.5 years with the bank. It paid well, it taught me great customer service and I made some amazing life long friends.

But it was soon time to take a look around and see what I wanted to do next - I had no ambitions to be bank manager, or to go into any other areas of the bank, so I decided to look around for the next thing for me.

I completely changed career and ended up in Market Research for a trendy agency near Holborn. Within my first week we were all taken to France for the day on a jolly, with fruits de mer and wine a plenty - it was certainly an eye opener and I revelled in the buzz and franticity of the advertising world. We worked with the likes of Saatchi and Saatchi, BMP and DDB and hosted the annual yacht race around Cowes and the Isle of Wight - it was a scene I'd never been part of but felt welcomed within and I loved it - seeing the passion and heights of achievement within the companies was contagious and whereas before I had thought of myself as not important enough to eat at some of the trendy restaurants in London, I actually realised that I did have a brain and something important to give too.

At one meeting with my boss and some suited and booted people at Saatchi and Saatchi, on what was the skype equivalent in those days (what they called a pizza) that connected London with the US, when everyone was using complicated words and trying to puff up what was being said - I sat there, as a 20 year old, thinking "is this what they are trying to say" and thinking would I look a fool if I said it? But then said "is this what you are trying to say" and they would say "yes, that's exactly it" and I would wonder why there was all the "fluff" and complications of the communication.

So from joining as receptionist, I resigned as Field Manager - I'd climbed a steep ladder in an amazing company that were a fantastic support for my ideas and suggestions. But, having just bought my first house, it was risky times at work and my salary cheque bounced, so, again, I had to look at where I wanted to progress from there. It was time to move on. And my boyfriend at the time had been in unsteady work, so it was my salary that was relied upon - so I looked around and was offered a job working for Warner Bros. in International Television. I was elated. This was going to be the best job ever.

It ended up being the most boring job for me ever! My boss was away a lot, we didn't have the internet, so I ended up offering my services to the marketing department and working with the head of marketing for shows such as Friends, ER and Superman. I did feel very foolish when I asked the Marketing Manager if those were "her friends" about a framed photo of the famous 6! Well Friends was not that famous then!

After 9 months, and when my boyfriend at the time got a longer contract (he worked in TV), the mortgage was not on my head for a few months, so again, it was time to go - I didn't know what I wanted to do so decided to temp for a while. A week at Estee Lauder was very interesting but what I loved about temping was being in control of my own destiny. If I didn't want to work that week, or for that particular company, I could decline.

After around 3 weeks of loving temping, I was offered a job at a marketing agency in North London. It was near to my home and with people I knew, so I was a bit fearful of feeling "retired" - I'd always worked in London - but I decided to go for it and see what happened.

I ended up meeting my gorgeous husband there and spending 13 years plus in marketing - working my way up to Marketing

Director and working with some amazing brands such as Veolia Water, Citilink, BBC and various energy companies.

It was when I had my children that everything changed - as it does for many women and parents. Like I say, I'd never wanted a career, I simply wanted to earn enough money to be independent and pay my own way in life - to have a roof over my head and to be able to afford lots of G&Ts ;)

But it all changed when I had my two gorgeous sons. With our first, Ernie, I had to go back to work. We'd just bought a big house in St Albans and we couldn't afford for me to give up. I went back 4 days a week and I remember crying in the kitchen as my 3 month old was in nursery or with grandparents - I wanted it to be me who was there for him.

When my second, Frankie, was born, more demand was put on me and at one point in our lives, we had a childminder picking them up from school and I was doing long hours.

It was my mum that said to me "you won't ever get this time back with the kids" that it really hit home. I'd started a dance class - dance routines to pop music, for women aged 18+ - learning dance routines to tracks from the 80s, 90s and 00s - I wanted to get active, shed a bit of baby weight and just have an hour of "me" time away from work and the demands of the kids.

I was getting more emails about Popdance than I was for my marketing job and I thought that this wasn't fair on my employer. So, decided to go for it. We couldn't afford it and we cut our household income in half by my leaving a well paid job - but it was my husband who said I should go for it and that this could be something amazing!

It was a massive decision, and one that financially on paper we would not have taken, but it's given me an amazing life - being able to be there for my kids, and for my parents and my husbands parents - to go sledging with the kids when it snows and catch up with work in the evening - to head to the pool when it's sunny and work there - to be able to work from anywhere in the world and be with the ones I love is incredible.

But it didn't just stop there!

From one dance class in St Albans, we were approached to run family Popdance classes in a Holiday Park, and then other dance teachers wanted to run Popdance, and then toddler classes were in demand, followed by birthday parties, hen parties, workshops with brownies and guides, after school clubs - it just escalated.

Now Popdance is international - and we work with amazing dance teachers across the globe - helping them to run successful and profitable Popdance classes, parties and events.

I still love going to Popdance every week - even though I'm not a dance teacher - I think that's what makes it work - enjoying being a customer of my own business - having the marketing skills and business skills to help others make a fantastic living out of Popdance, and working with our teachers as a team - we are all amazing at something, but we are all not amazing at everything - sharing our skills and support is what makes it work.

And that's how we led on to St Albans Businesses - having never run a business before, it was a massive learning curve. Feeling alone, nervous, could I do it!? And meeting other amazing people running, starting, heading up their businesses, made a massive difference to me - support, help and collaboration were the instigation of SAB and it's the driving force behind what makes Popdance the fantastic, ambitious, driven and passionate business that it is.

Find your drive, go for it and never, never, never give up!

SUE WYBROW
www.popdanceworld.com

IAN AND MELANIE WOODING-JONES

Redbourn Auto Solutions

Redbourn Auto Solutions

Setting up your own business sounds so easy on paper, even exciting, but no-one explains the impact on you and your family when faced with so many challenges on a daily basis. So, here is the truth about setting up an SME: the highs, the lows and our motivation to keep going.

Setting up

We've gained a vast expanse of knowledge through many years' experience in different franchised main dealerships. This exposed the challenges faced by operating under a manufacturer, most importantly how a large corporation makes profit (sales – costs = profit).

To increase sales, staff are incentivised through targets which are heavily bonused. This gives rise to the temptation of overselling such as reporting car faults a little early than necessary, or finding fault in an MOT to repair, or upselling a service plan which doesn't cover wear and tear. There are many different ways garages optimise their income. We are different.

The desire to be able to deliver excellent customer service in a transparent and honest way became an opportunity we were compelled to pursue. We wanted to compete with the best. An independent garage, changing common perceptions by delivering high quality service and exacting standards, providing a real alternative to a main dealer.

Whilst delivering this, we also wanted to spend more time together as a family. With 4 growing children, finding quality time to be with them was essential.

Ian ran the local Saab dealerships and, in 2012 when Saab met its demise, it presented the perfect opportunity to set up a repair centre. Ian continued to work and Melanie provided a joint role bringing up the children and supporting a new business. A highly competent Service Manager, a Technician and an Apprentice were appointed. Saab parts stock were purchased from the Administrators which paid the rent and staff for the first 6 months whilst planning permission was sought.

The Planning Nightmare

At the time, the Government were driving the growth of SME's, so we didn't expect red tape to prevent us from opening. An inability to be able to talk to someone at St Albans District Council led to numerous submissions being made. We even attended a Redbourn Parish Council Planning meeting to gain their support. The neighbouring units on the Industrial Estate were also obstructive as we became tarred with the same brush as many independents. After submitting an 80-page document responding to all objections and countering those that we anticipated, we were eventually granted change of use and opened as Redbourn Auto Solutions on 11 July 2012.

However, the 6 months it took to open had a significant negative impact on our financial plan, made worse when the Landlord increased the rent because we were an automotive business.

We sought bank support, but because we had already started trading (in parts) and making a loss, the bank would only give us minimal support. If we had approached them before trading, they would have offered more support... it was a tough lesson to learn.

With the support of friends and family, we progressed to purchasing new vehicle lifts and specialist equipment.

Know your customer

There's no point dedicating time and energy attracting the wrong customers. It leads to frustration and dissatisfaction. You can't please everyone, so identifying your own customer is essential. We needed customers who understood good quality service, appreciated the high level of capability we can offer, who respected honesty and trusted judgements being made.

There are many garages offering 'deals for cash' or those who fit cheap parts to lower their costs, but we wanted to be different and unwilling to compromise our standards (cheap parts often don't fit properly, wear prematurely or break). We wanted to trade honestly and have faith in our staff's abilities and in the parts we were supplying.

We deal with many different vehicles from milk floats, horse boxes, classics and transits to Aston Martin, Porsche and Ferrari! So, our customer base is wide and varied, but they all understand quality and good customer service.

Customer feedback has been important to shaping our business: We originally set up as a Saab specialist, but our customers owned cars from a variety of manufacturer. So, we broadened our technical knowledge and bought in diagnostic equipment to cope with the emerging demands.

Our geographic demographic expanded into Harpenden and St Albans, so we provided courtesy cars and collection and delivery service for our customers convenience.

Some customers had 4x4's and light commercial vehicles, so we purchased larger vehicle lifts to cope with this demand. Our customers said they would like tyres from a trusted supplier, so we provided tyres from budget to performance tyres and added 4-wheel alignment.

We became the first garage in Hertfordshire to gain the Trading Standards mark and Which accreditation.

We streamlined processes to ensure efficiency in every area of the business ensuring customers received their cars back quickly, which was especially important for our corporate clients. It ranged from working with suppliers to ensure the correct parts arrived on time, to allocating areas of responsibility to secure a clean and tidy workshop.

Stunning Staff

We've always believed in employing people who are better than we are, but in desperation when work flow was peaking we recruited in haste. It was the only year our upward financials took a dip whilst we 'moved-on' those who were harming our business. We changed our recruitment process and stayed firm in our requirements. We also took the opportunity to benchmark our salaries and benefits. Now we have the best team! Highly qualified Technicians from Master to Apprentice, with skills that complement each other. Above all, we all understand the importance of exceptional customer service, because we all have similar backgrounds.

Flaming Finance

We both came from backgrounds where we managed budgets. The notable difference is that it was someone else's money! Setting up a new business is about risk taking and financially this can be a difficult decision to make. It's the bit that prevents starting up, continued progression and in some cases businesses fold... and cash flow is usually the cause.

The first few years were not easy. We borrowed, sold our cars, and certainly didn't pay ourselves. The children regularly ate beans on toast and family shipped in the odd monthly shopping. We couldn't afford to go out... not even to the local pub.

Holidays were a thing of the past. The hardest thing was losing friends. We couldn't afford to go out and so their lives continued without us. We had to make the most of what we had and the children got involved in the business. Cleaning, sorting, filing, litter picking... our lives centred around the business. Our house was on the line, so we had to make it work.

5 years on, and the business remains in debt but is moving forward at unprecedented levels year on year with significant profit increases.

What's next?

We're continuing to grow! We've moved from a customer base of zero in 2012, to welcoming over 10,800 cars through the door. Customer satisfaction and retention is high. We've seen an increase in commercial business, tyres, and in the variety of vehicle we look after, welcoming more prestigious vehicles than before. We haven't let a recent rent increase of 40% hold us back. It's just another challenge to overcome.

We'll continue to go where our customers take us, without compromising our high Standards.

Conclusion

We love what we do! We're achieving our aspirations and have our own successful business. We offer a sensible alternative to a main dealer and our customers receive honest feedback on their cars with no overselling. We even write articles for local magazines on car related topics.

We have planned our first holiday as a family in 5 years (it's only a week, but it's a start) and we're working on daily family time.

We've met many people on our journey who have helped us on the way. They may not necessarily understand their profound impact on our business. It could have been a comment by a friend, thoughts from a networking meeting or a chance read.

Our recommendations to you are:

Have a clear vision of what you want to achieve and how you're going to get there, but be prepared to change.

Don't get distracted! Hold tight to the belief you have in your business. You'll face many hurdles, but dealing with them will make you stronger.

Build a network of people who will support you. There will be plenty to hold you back.

Understand that everyone has their own views. Just because you've started a new venture, doesn't mean that everyone will change to accommodate you!

Be brave. If an opportunity presents itself, take the risk and work it out later.

Be genuine. Be yourself.

Above all... don't look back! Keep moving forwards.

IAN AND MELANIE
WOODING-JONES
www.redbournautosolutions.co.uk

SARAH LOMAX

Holiday Inn Express St Albans

I guess the story would start for me in January 2016. I was lucky enough to be appointed for the position of Sales Manager working on the opening of the brand-new Holiday Inn Express St Albans! Previously to that I had been working for a different management company, looking after Sales in many of the Holiday Inn Express properties in the North of England. Remote working was not for me as I like to give a personal service and get to know all the guests and clients. To say that I wanted the Sales Manager job in a brand-new hotel would be a massive understatement. I wanted something that I could really get my teeth into, get to know the local market, people and generally be part of a community. Cut forward a month and I had my first site visit!

A cold and sunny January morning, myself and the General Manager donned our hard hats to see the hotel for the first. I fell in love instantly. She was cold, she was muddy and she had no windows but she was fabulous.   There is something very special about working on the opening of a hotel. It is all about the 'firsts' First interior walls, first windows. The hotel and business was my baby!

Then the hard work truly began, to go out and sell a vision and concept. Armed with a power point presentation, an artist impression of what the hotel was going to look like and some cupcakes I was off. Looking back, I think that was the most enjoyable part of it for me. In my head, I had a vision and to go around and building up excitement about it was great. My life became living out of the boot of the car whilst waiting for the hotel (and office) to open, as did working from various coffee shops trying to find quiet, coffee and Wi-Fi. Not as easy as you might think!

After a couple of pushbacks, due to the building works running over, we were ready to open. The hotel was signed off by our brand Wednesday 20th July and we opened the doors! We had our first booking straight away and our first guests within the hour. All systems were go!

The incredible feedback about our product and guest service has motivated us even further. We have just had the First Birthday celebrations with the hotel in operation for a full year. It has far exceeded all our expectations both as a business and our concept of what we wanted it to be.

SARAH LOMAX
www.ihg.com/holidayinnexpress/
hotels/gb/en/st-albans/ltnst/
hoteldetail

JENNY FORD
Author of inspirational books
for adults and children

My journey started quite a few years ago when I decided to go on a free Nail Art course. It was only once a week, in a community centre in Hatfield and was run by Oaklands College. There was no qualification given but you got a certificate to say that you had attended the course. I had never really been that interested in nails before. I had three beautiful children to take care of so my nails, nor anyone else's, were simply not on my list of priorities! But I also wanted to do something for me, so I thought, why not give it a go? I would practise on family and friends and discovered that I was actually enjoying it, plus I was pretty good at it if I do say so myself!

After finishing the course, my friends would say to me, "Why don't you get qualified properly and do it for a living?" But how could I? I had three children to take care of. It did get me thinking though. I did some research and found that I could do a City and Guilds Manicure and Pedicure qualification at Watford College, every Saturday for six months. By this time in my life, I was classed as a 'mature' student and found myself amongst a classroom of 17-18 year olds. Whilst this didn't concern me, there was one thing that did and that was when it came to doing the theory exams. I was dreading them. You see, I was not the best student at school; actually, I was never at school. I was a

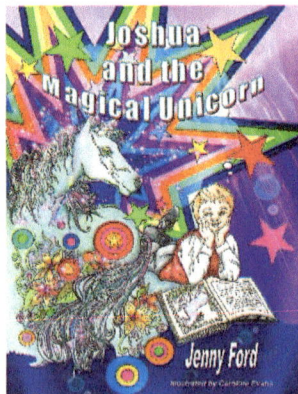

bit of a rebel. I would walk in one gate and straight out the other (not something I am proud of), so my education was not the best. I convinced myself that I was going to fail.

After six months the course came to an end and it was then a very long wait for the results. The day had come. The letter landed on the floor but I couldn't open it; my husband had to read it. When he told me my results I could have cried. Well, I did actually cry! I had gained a Distinction in Practical and Theory.

I thought they had made a mistake, so I spoke to my tutor who confirmed that the results were correct. I went on to do further training in beauty treatments and that was the start of my career as a Beauty Therapist. I decided not to go into a salon as I still had my children to think about, so I became self-employed as a mobile therapist which enabled me to work around them. I loved my job and worked very hard.

Over the years I managed to build up an excellent client base and ran a very successful business. One of my clients was singer, Radio 2 and TV presenter, Amazon No. 1 bestselling author, and business coach, Janey Lee Grace. Things were looking good. Until the day my whole world fell to pieces, when I was diagnosed with Multiple Sclerosis. Why, how, why me? All these questions ran through my head. It wasn't just me going through it but also my family and my children. I had to give up my business as I couldn't drive anymore, I was too tired to even get out of bed some days and eventually, the business I had worked so hard to build had gone. Just like that. Was that it for me?

After years of feeling sorry for myself and being angry and depressed, I was introduced to meditation which completely changed my life. It changed the way I looked at things; I became more focused and more at peace within myself, and that's when my writing journey began. No-one was more surprised than me when I wrote my first book, given my educational background (or lack of)! I was never interested in reading or writing, not even as a child; it literally just happened. Perhaps you could call it divine intervention!

I was chuffed to pieces when it was published. It gave me the push that I needed to get my life back to as normal as it possibly could. I then wrote another book, and another, and then my first children's book. I was on a roll.

Where was all of this coming from? It was then that I realised I was an author! Who would have ever believed it? I know my teachers certainly wouldn't have...

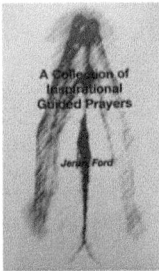

My local radio station (Radio Verulam 92.6FM) invited me for an interview to talk about my books and I've been there ever since. I now co-present and produce on one of the shows and have also recently adapted one of my books into a play, which I am hoping will be produced one day.

I have gone from having a thriving business to falling into a deep, dark place but have come out the other end, happier than I have ever been. I have started all over again in a new career, which I never imagined was possible. I truly believe that writing is my true life's purpose! I am continually inspired and gain motivation by the different people that I meet every day which drives me to be the best that I can.

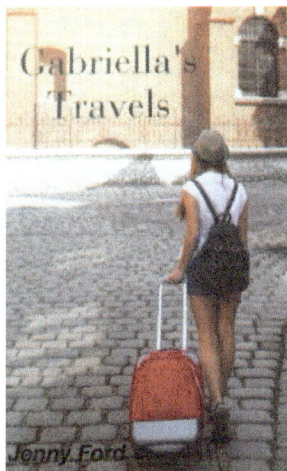

Running your own business can be hard work at times but one that I would highly recommend as long as you stay focused, grounded and have that passion. Never give up when you are faced with challenges; trust, believe and have faith. I am so truly blessed, grateful and thankful for the life I have. Without the knocks and hard times I wouldn't be where I am today. Positive thinking leads to positive results and if it happened to me it can happen to you.

My first business award very recently presented to me by St Albans Businesses is absolute testament to that.

JENNY FORD
www.jennyfordauthor.com

TOULA AND JAMES MESSER

The Sultans of Swag™

○ **SAATCHI ART**

This is a true story. Some of the characters' names may have been changed to protect the innocent.

Many of you may know our names; you may even know that we sell our own awesome photographic wall art prints, gifts and home decor but not many of you know the hows and whys of how this came to be.

My name is Toula Mavridou-Messer and I am a photographer. I am married to James Messer and he is a graphic designer/ illustrator and digital artist. Together we run The Sultans of Swag™. However, it wasn't always like this.

In the beginning, I was a PR. I started helping on campaigns for London clubs when I was 13, during the school holidays, after school and at weekends.

At 15, I co-wrote a regular gossip column for Gay News with my best friend Jane Goldman and even had to leave my English 'O' level early to go and interview Divine at Zandra Rhodes home in Notting Hill.

Then came the Bros years. I was their personal manager and stylist and based the Bros 'look' on a picture of a 10 year old boy that I saw in a Next catalogue on the way to Cuts in Soho, where the boys finally had their long golden locks shorn into shape, despite their protests.

By the age of 19, I had set up my own entertainments PR firm - P.R. Inc. (after having worked on campaigns for the late George Michael and various other big 80s names including: Pepsie & Shirlie, Sid Haywoode, Blue Mercedes and even Great Train Robber Ronnie Biggs) and was the youngest principal of any PR firm world-wide, according to The Guinness Book of Records.

At P.R. Inc. we looked after Shirley Bassey, Eric Clapton, 5-Star, Anderson Bruford Wakeman Howe (formerly Yes)...and a number of very big UK charities.

Through circumstance and choice, I moved from PR into TV and was part of the GMTV start-up. After a year of overnights and early mornings my body demanded an easier schedule, so instead I ended up building a hospital in Romania in 54 hours for Challenge Anneka and eventually found myself working on The Golden Globe Awards, American Music Awards, People's Choice Awards and various other crazy exciting entertainment shows in Hollywood, where I also looked after many of the biggest names in the world.

Those incredibly famous names (ones who even my grandmother would know) included: Sophia Loren, Al Pacino,

Robert De Niro and Martin Scorsese. Fortunately, I also worked with some of the more 'modern' ones, such as: Johnny Depp, Brad Pitt, Angelina Jolie and Leonardo DiCaprio...!

In between visas, I set up the UK's first and best celebrity gifting company The Sultans of Swag™ (gifting celebs at events such as the BRITs, Royal Variety Performance, British Comedy Awards and so on). I also met and married James. It was a good time.

Then the 2008 recession hit and it was time for us to move on to pastures new, as gifting items to celebrities was no longer included on budgets.

Those pastures were based in Studio City in LA. James used his artistic and design skills to work as part of the art production teams on a number of extremely high profile commercials, featuring stars such as: Jay Leno, Cameron Diaz and Breaking Bad's Bryan Cranston. James even stood in for the 'Happy' singer Pharrell, too!

We were in LA when the call came on December 4th, 2014, that Mum's husband had died and within less than 30 minutes we were booked on return flights home. My beautiful Mother has dementia and Alzheimer's and needed us here, so of course we didn't hesitate.

Life hasn't been and still isn't easy. When you move, other people also move on - so, you know that it's time to really search your soul to find your next path and adding awesome swagger to people's lives is as clear to us as the Yellow Brick Road was to Dorothy!

For us, finding the path was easy - it was all lit up with sparkly fairy-lights and neon arrows pointing the way (you may have seen my photographs of them). In other words, our hearts chose the path for us.

Art is how your heart sees things, right? Well, our hearts wanted to share some of what we have seen and hope that hearts around the world respond. It's early days but things are falling into place and for me that's a big sign that the Universe is on our side and that the time is now.

All of my photographs have been taken on an ancient Nikon - it's my pride and joy. It's the camera that took the pictures that Saatchi curated into collections and made me into a Saatchi Recognised Artist.

In just a few short months we have achieved a great deal and will continue to build on that foundation.

A selection of our art has been licensed in the USA and is now available for sale through some of their biggest outlets there, such as Wayfair, Walmart, Houzz, Overstock and Better Homes &Gardens. We aim to match and exceed that level of success here in the UK, too. In the meantime, we are thrilled to be exhibiting locally at the Nude Tin Can Gallery and recently at both DST Design and at the first birthday of the Holiday Inn, St Alban's, when the lovely Sarah Lomax invited us to showcase our prints after seeing them in all of their glory at the Woohoos.

Sales are coming in at all ends of the budget-spectrum. We have even been inundated with requests for custom orders for enormous sized prints for office wall art and even large shiny aluminium prints for surprise landmark birthdays and special events.

The best thing of all is that we get to travel and share our visual treasures and know that some of those treasures are in people's homes all around the world bringing happiness and evoking heartfelt memories to those who now own them.

TOULA AND JAMES MESSER
www.TheSultansofSwag.Etsy.com

MONIR ALI
PHOTOGRAPHER

Commercial Photographer, Little Big Ego, Asian Wedding Experience, Portobello Picture Co and Village Workspace.

After a colourful career spanning various job roles from Classified Sales Executive, Account Manager for a small PR and marketing firm, to Account Director, Media Planner, Head of Marketing for a TV channel, Regional Director of a consultancy company to my last role as a Special Projects Manager for a publishing house, I wanted to be able to work to live rather than live to work.

While working for the publishing house I explored an old skill I had, which I had originally wanted to follow out of university; Photography. However, at the time a lack of funds and a lack of support from organisations like the PYT had meant I had to put that part of my life on hold. After some time, a few friends found out about my skill and asked me to photograph some weddings, reluctantly I accepted. To my surprise I really enjoyed it and realised that this could be fun.

With the support of my wife, Monica, I gathered enough courage to send my boss my resignation letter, borrowed some money from my family and bought my first digital camera. I printed some flyers at home and got ready for the start of the new career I dreamt of.

Struggles are part and parcel of being your own boss, but ours started on day one of the business – when I found out we were going to be blessed with a child. The pressure was on; not only did we not have a regular income which was bad enough, we had also just purchased our first home too. So, the heat was on. I struggled to get clients, I was driving around Manchester meeting clients and doing stuff for free before we got any results. Marketing to a niche market is difficult at the best of times, but when there are no other vehicles to promote your business what do you do, you create one. So, with a friend we developed a second business, The Asian Wedding Experience.

Being in business for ten years is probably my biggest achievement as I have never stayed in a job for more than three years at a time, so this is the longest job I have ever held. The highlight of my career was being awarded a WOOHOO, in 2017 which now sits alongside my other awards.

The freedom of working to live, and the thousands of people I have met along the way, and most importantly the learning experiences I have had has made me a more rounded individual. My work has allowed me to travel around the world for people and businesses that value my skill set which has made my life a lot more hectic than it ever was before. One of the downsides is we never switch off, and as the business is technically a family business, which involves Monica and the two girls, Amelia and Arianna, THEY are the key to the success of the business.

It's surprising how astute and honest six and nine year olds are. All major business decisions are discussed with the girls over a hot chocolate and once even at a teddy bear picnic. But with that also comes the down side of the business where I don't get to see them as much as I would like.

Naturally success is the motivator behind what we do, and that allows for us to be content in our lives with family and friends. For different people, success means different things, but for me it's a combination of family, friends and being able to live a little.

If you are thinking about starting your own business, think hard, talk to others, shadow a self-employed person, look at the down sides and then look at the upsides. For years I was working from the kitchen table, lost touch with friends and hardly went out at all because I wanted the business to be a success. Remember to keep things in perspective.

MONIR ALI PHOTOGRAPHER
www.monirali.com

KRISTINA SNARSKIENE

Bee Divine Beauty Therapist

Whilst working in the hospitality industry I had true passion for helping and developing people, which led me into studying beauty. After qualifying as a beauty therapist I decided to leave my sales carrier in central London and move to the beauty industry.

My beauty career started at the Spa at Mandarin Oriental in London, where I gained a great knowledge of customer service and the highest standards of treatments.

When my son started school, due to commute into London, I had to relocate my work to St Albans. That's when I started working at the local spa. I've always worked with a goal to one day work for myself and provide the highest quality of service and treatments that I felt was needed in the industry.

In May 2016 the treatment room at Alley Cats became available and it was opportunity that I couldn't say no to! Of course I thought there are so many salons and beauty therapists in St Albans, is there a place for me? But after careful consideration I left my job and started working for myself.

And never looked back! I love working the hours that I set for myself to work around children and love the flexibility of my work. My core desire is to make people look and feel great in their bodies by providing the highest quality treatments. I don't compete with anybody apart from myself. I'm proud to say that the treatments that I provide to my clients are highly personalised. I love that my clients can escape the outside world and hide away for few hours to take some time out for themselves. As I believe self-care is very important and plays a big role in self-confidence. A lot of the time my work doesn't feel like work because I meet so many lovely people. It's a very social job.

My biggest reward is my happy clients that come back and recommend me to their friends.

A few months into the business I have realised that running your own business is not that simple. I found myself having to cover the roles of accountant, buyer, marketing person, graphic designer and my own role of a beauty therapist! And as much as I enjoy all the beauty treatments and feel very happy doing them, I find myself struggling with the rest of the business side. Over the past year I have learnt that sometimes it's best to outsource the jobs that I'm not specialised in and takes a lot of my time and concentrate what I do best, which is providing treatments to my clients.

Now, over a year into running my own business I look back and feel really proud how far I have come. I often forget that my business is still a little baby and needs looking after and nurturing. It's only the beginning of my adventure and I look forward what the future brings for me.

KRISTINA SNARSKIENE
www.beedivinehairremoval.co.uk

ATLAS CLARE SUTTIE
Atlas Translations Ltd

Twenty two years old, no money, a background in sales of everything from anti-wrinkle cream and computer software to telephone switchboard systems. I'd waited on tables, cleaned apartments, flipped burgers in a remote outback roadhouse and checked for rogue sunflowers in crops in the Australian desert. I'd even been a bank manager! But what now?

I had loved languages at school, and studied a bit of linguistics, but had steered away from this career path as my older sister was a translator. Then I temped at a translation agency in Cambridge and thought, "I could do this - better!"

It was 1991, it was a recession, but a night in a pub with my friend and we cobbled together a business plan and a name – Atlas Translations – it had to begin with A to be near the top of the Yellow Pages listing. And yes, Aardvark Translations already existed.

We found a tiny office above Lloyds Bank, filled it with office furniture from a skip at a local business park and donations from kind friends, gave the room a lick of paint, and we were off. Our first logo was a green bicycle – we were in Cambridge and delivered leaflets locally on our bikes. And I can't draw.

That was 26 years ago and I still love this business. So much has changed – the internet arrived, my business partner left, staff have come and gone, there have been difficult times.

Back in the last century, location really mattered for a service like Atlas, and we had couriers coming and going with work. Having an office in Covent Garden in London helped us serve our clients, even though I was commuting from St Albans after 1998. Whenever our lease came up for renewal I was too scared to move the office out of London, until finally in 2012 I took the plunge and really, I should have done it years before. In a smaller city it is easier to find and keep staff, and the local business community is phenomenal. As I live in St Albans with a young family, my quality of life has also improved.

It's hard to squash 26 years into 1000 words, but here's some of what I've picked up along the way.

Bad times

Taking out a business loan on a fixed rate of interest at the height of a recession. Interest rates have NEVER been higher since. But without that loan, we couldn't have started. So maybe that should be under good!

Good times

Winning contracts, watching staff develop. Starting our work placement scheme in 1992 and having over 175 interns passing through our training programme. Becoming ISO certified and passing every external annual audit since. Learning to delegate

work and employing some fantastic staff and managers.

Advice

Take advice! You may well be offered lots of conflicting advice. I knew nothing about computers, or accounting and made sure these areas were looked after by experts. Move with the times. Working practices, IT, telephony – it all changes so fast and you will need to keep up with it. Concentrate on the bits you are good at that bring in the revenue, and delegate the small stuff to allow you to do this. Recognise your weaknesses and delegate, or ask for help and address them.

Memories

Coming in after the weekend and finding pages and pages of curled up fax paper. The first time the phone rang and it wasn't my mum. Our first job, and the cheque we received for our first invoice.

Meetings, exhibitions, inspiring clients and exceptionally talented translators.

Be kind

To staff, to clients, to suppliers, and to yourself. Everyone has bad days, everyone makes mistakes. In most industries, this isn't the end of the world. Say sorry and see what can be done to rectify any mistakes or misunderstandings. You might be surprised how much someone can appreciate this and it can turn a bad situation around.

Be a Leader

That's a bit biz-speak for me, but stand out in your industry as someone who helps those starting out, who shares information and educates.

Go Local

Discover your local business community. Why buy your stationery from the other side of the country when there's probably a local supplier just up the road? Meet up with other local businesses and you'll find a wealth of skills, knowledge and services on your doorstep.

Take time out

Tricky when starting out, especially if you're working alone; but you need a holiday. Think of ways to cover your absence with an answering service or a great virtual assistant to take calls and let you know if there is that all important phone call you've been waiting for!

Have understanding friends

Atlas is my baby, very precious and special to me. Friends and family have shared the good and bad times and provided a sounding board. If you find you're always moaning about the same problem, it's probably time to sort it out one way or another.

Make difficult decisions – without delaying

There will be some to make. Redundancies, ending contracts, unpleasant tasks. There's no point in delaying.

Avoid high heels

If you can't walk in them. I really, really can't. I attended a meeting at a major pharmaceutical company and fell down some stairs rather spectacularly just before the purchasing team came to greet me. I was able to hobble towards them trying to hide what had just happened, and we did win the contract; I had some spectacular bruises as souvenirs for weeks after.

Be yourself (see high heels)

We all like to deal with genuine people so there's just no point in pretending to be someone you are not.

Learn to say no

In many areas of life, including business, it's easy to say yes to all requests and then become bogged down with too much to do, some of it things you didn't really want to do but were too polite to say. Learn to say politely say No, and stop – don't apologise or justify it. You can't do everything.

But also learn to say yes

Do step out of the old faithful comfort zone, you may surprise yourself! Naked Christmas cards, fire walking, joining a new group, whatever it is. Challenge yourself.

Grow. Have staff

It's a big step taking on a member of staff. But it may be just what you need to grow your business. And to give you the freedom to do more of what you're best at. If you're not sure, offer a short term or temporary contract and see how it goes.

Make mistakes in your business

Well, not deliberately! But accept that you probably will make a mistake every now and again. Look, learn and move along.

Have a plan and keep planning

When you think about starting a business, everyone tells you that you must have a business plan. So you put one together, but of course as you progress further, plans will change, you'll learn and you may even completely change direction. Keep an eye on the future – and update your plan regularly.

Make a profit

This is the point, and it's worth saying.

CLARE SUTTIE
www.atlas-translations.co.uk

MARIAN MURPHY

Flourish with Social Media

I established my business is June 2013. For 7 years prior to that I had been a stay at home mum to my two boys – something I feel fortunate to have been able to do. Towards the latter part of 2012 it was time to re-enter the workforce.

In the Summer of 2012, a month before my youngest son was starting school I went home to Ireland on holiday with the family. Before we got on the ferry to come back to the UK my husband presented me with a present, a book called 'Flourishing by Maureen Gaffney', a clinical psychologist and Professor at University College Dublin. My husband encouraged me to write something on the book which I did. It read '4th August 2012 – Ferry at Holyhead back from holidays in Ireland – I am going to flourish!'

In September, I received an email from the agency Ten2Two who had a coach offering 6 pro bono coaching sessions. Not knowing what coaching was about, I decided it could be a useful exercise so I expressed my interest. I was put in contact with Allison Spargo, MD of People For The Future.

I went to the coaching sessions with an open mind and was blown away by what I achieved over 6 sessions. At the time, the 'social media for business' area was being talked about a lot. With a Degree in Business and a background in business development and sales I could really see how social media was going to be the next revolution. And even more key to this was that I felt I would not be at a disadvantage to others in this arena as the area was so new and evolving. The big advantage of social media was that it was levelling the playing field between small and large businesses.

Creativity and building relationships would be just as important as budget. I loved the fact that a small business would have the exact same tools as a multinational at their disposal. I was hooked.

After my first coaching session, I decided to learn as much as possible about the social media area and devoured everything social media for the following 9 months. In Dec 2012, I wrote an article 'Give Your Business Some TLC – Tweet, Like, Connect. This article was published by Socialmediopolis an American website with a huge social media community (LinkedIn 1,275,000). This was my first time getting an article published and I viewed it as a huge achievement and a sign I was on the right track.

In April 2013, I went for an interview for a social media role. This was a defining moment for me. I came out of the interview feeling I was as knowledgeable as the person interviewing me. This was the moment I decided I would set up my own business. I played around with lots of ideas on the business name but the word 'Flourish' kept popping up in my head. When I had an informal chat with my coach Allison, she said she thought this was a great name as I had flourished so much in the previous 9 months, through learning about social media. Layered on top of this, I wanted my clients to 'flourish with social media'. That was it - Flourish With Social Media was born.

I established my company & published my website within weeks. My initial plan was to offer social media management to businesses who needed a resource. This quickly evolved and I found over the years training & empowering my clients has been where my true passion lies. I know I can give my clients the confidence and excitement to use social media to promote their business.

My focus initially was to start building up a great reputation. I felt if I did everything well and went above and beyond the call the duty, my reputation would grow and people would refer me. This strategy has really worked for me. I have 100% client satisfaction and I am getting referred by word of mouth and on social media regularly.

Flourish With Social Media presents
'CONTENT ON SOCIAL MEDIA WORKSHOP'
GETTING YOUR BUSINESS NOTICED IN THE MARKETPLACE

There have been struggles along the way. As I had never worked in the UK and had recently moved to Hertfordshire, I did not have a network of friends, ex-colleagues etc to draw from. I was starting literally from zero. There were times I wanted to give up but had great support to tell me 'keep going, you're doing great'. I joined WIBN, Women In Business Network in St Albans in January 2014 which was a great decision. After visiting lots of networking groups WIBN was the right one for me for so many reasons, I met lots of great businesswomen who were very supportive, had great ideas, and referred me to their network where possible.

There have been many achievements to date including:

- Seeing my clients literally skip out of my office after having a training session because of what they have learn.

- Every positive client testimonial

- Seeing the Facebook following of one of my client increase by over 2000 people over the past year due to a Facebook Page Review I carried out.

- Getting Certified Professional on Hootsuite, the social media dashboard.

- Becoming a social media advisor with the PR team managing the 2016 Irish General Election Campaign for a first-time candidate. This resulted in the candidate becoming the 1st woman in history to be elected in her constituency.

- Being asked to write a chapter on Networking on Twitter for the book 'How to Network Your Way To Success'.

- Being invited to become a founder member of the Social Media Marketing Society – a community of approx. 4000 social media marketers around the globe.

- Creating and delivering social media workshops to my clients.

- Being invited to become a speaker on social media for the Herts CIPD.

What I find most satisfying about running my own business is that I am creating something unique and that I can adapt to changing conditions in the social media space quickly by keeping up with new tools and techniques. I find the social media space so exciting and I love bringing new tools, apps and platforms to my client's attention. When I am managing social media for a client I can literally work from anywhere in the world, with my phone – that is a huge bonus!

I also like the fact that I can control the times I work, it does not mean I work less but I have the flexibility to do things I want to do e.g. I am a member of a choir in Harpenden who meet every Thursday from 2-3. I also volunteer with Harpenden Helping Hands, an organisation who assists the elderly or those who are not mobile get to the doctor, supermarket etc. I never have to miss anything my kids are involved in including assemblies, matches, day trips, plays, sports days etc.

Since setting up my own business my life has changed in many ways, I have a renewed sense of confidence in myself and my ability. I know I have something unique to offer that no one else can emulate – we all do! I have met many new business contacts & friends who are all very valuable tome. I am earning from something I have created myself – a nice feeling!

If you are thinking of setting up a business I would advise you to be patient, things do not happen as quickly as you expect. If you are going from a full-time job do as much of the planning and setting up before you give up your job. If you need money coming in, work part-time so you have the space and time to start building your business. Keep all business cards of people you meet so you can build your email list when you are ready. Get testimonials from people you have previously worked with or do some pro bono work to build up reviews on your website. Use these reviews when sending quotations or proposals to prospective clients – it gives them an extra hook to choose you. Set up templates for invoices, quotations etc as you will be repeating a lot of the same tasks so this will cut down time.

Don't undersell yourself at the start. Study the market for what you are offering and stick with that. If you start low, it's hard to go up.

MARIAN MURPHY

www.flourishwithsocialmedia.co.uk

HANNAH KNIGHT
HK Accountancy Services

Breaking the stereotype

HK Accountancy Services wasn't part of my 'life plan'. I wasn't one of those children who made it to year 7 of secondary school knowing who I wanted to be and what I wanted to do with my life.

I was never athletic; I wasn't the most popular and didn't (or so I thought) have any particular subject that I flourished in. That was until the third year of secondary school, when one of my mentors thankfully pointed out to me an ability to express myself and a high level of numeracy were my strengths. I shall forever be grateful for that advice.

I was a very fast learner and enjoyed it, despite the fact that I played up in class. I have a photographic memory for numbers (namely boys phone numbers back then) and an analytical mind, I can problem solve and rationalise most things.

After having my son, I took these strengths and decided that I needed to somehow make a career out of them. I gained my first qualifications and began my journey in 2006. I started to practice as a bookkeeper whilst studying for further accountancy qualifications, before forming my company.

Not long into my new career, I was given the chance to join a networking group run by a well-known national organisation, to get to know others in my own and similar professions and was invited to join them at an event.

I walked into the venue in a knee length black dress, red and purple hair and covered in tattoos. I fought my way through a sea of men in grey and black suits and suddenly wondered if I'd ended up in the wrong function room, someone's wake perhaps? I earwigged for a while and came to the grim realisation that I was in the right place. Fast forward 2 hours, after listening to lots of arrogance, back patting and tax jargon that I wasn't yet up to speed with, and feeling completely out of my depth, I had a conversation with a group of fellow accountants and then left in tears.

I am not cut out for this, I thought, I can't be like this. I love my career and have found something that not only am I good at but passionate about too, but I just cannot conform to be the type of person that they expect me to be.

I took the next couple of weeks gathering my thoughts and decided to do some market research. What do people look for in an accountant? What puts people off from employing an accountant? What do individuals actually think accountants do?

The results shocked me.

I realised at this point I was in fact doing everything right. I was being the person that I am, a human being, working for other human beings, doing something that I'm good at which helps them. They have their areas of expertise and I have mine. I always try to not be judgmental; I don't want to take over people's businesses and finances, as it appears people believe accountants do. I wanted to help people, particularly those new to business and I also wanted to study to ensure I knew every relief, allowance and loophole available to these people because that is what they want and need from me.

I furthered my education in 2013 and gained an accounting degree in the USA so that I could practice internationally, which was a huge step for me as an individual but also for my practice. I took on an employee and since then my company has grown from strength to strength - I found our key strengths and turned these into areas of expertise. We also continuously educate ourselves to ensure we are always up to date with the latest legislation and regulations.

As for the future of HK Accountancy Services, I have always said, and stick by this, that I don't ever wish to become a huge accountancy firm. I run a home based practice, and even now with over 300 clients, I know all by first name and do not wish for any client to ever become a client reference.

I have built my business based on what clients want and need in an accountant, not on the stereotype that surrounds us. I owe my success to the very people I am working for. I am fortunate enough to work for some of the most interesting and diverse people I've ever had the pleasure of knowing and they appreciate what I do for them.

I am extremely proud of where I am now, not arrogant, just overwhelmed. I wasn't born with a silver spoon and I really had to dig through a lot of mud to get where I am. I found that working with clients who have been introduced via word of mouth has worked best for my business as people know what to expect from me – that being a professional, ethical, knowledgeable service without the stigma attached.

The flattering and sometimes funny reviews and testimonials I receive from my clients really do go to show how they feel about me; I've been labelled a queen accountant, epic tax adviser, an awesome person and even a crazy cat lady (believe me, it's totally relevant to my character). These compliments make the stresses of working in a high-pressure role and environment all the more worth it.

My tip to all of those who are new in business is, no matter the profession, don't live up to the stereotypes, be who you are, offer the best service possible and your clients' satisfaction will continue to reward you. I have come to learn in the last 10 years that the networking event that I was invited to, was actually not very typical. I have since met, worked with and become friends with some amazing individuals, both in my own field and similar professions and they are some of the best people I know.

We are all the same, we all struggle, we all have down days, none of us are perfect.

Just be who you are, doing what you're good at.

HANNAH KNIGHT
www.hk-accountancy.co.uk

Hey mic! STEVE CLARKE

EurekaSelling **Eureka Selling & Hey Mic!**

As is often the case with entrepreneurs around the world, I wasn't gripped or inspired by formal education. I didn't go to college or study at university, in fact I left school at the age of 16 with no career path or obvious opportunities ahead.

Having reached the lofty heights of petrol pump attendant at the age of 18 I was simply not prepared to just accept the hand I'd been dealt. I became engrossed in the power of personal development and goal setting. By my 19th birthday with a "yes I can" attitude and determination to succeed I found my niche in sales.

And to be frank... I was pretty good at it.

I don't know why people over complicate sales - be nice to more people, be genuine and help solve problems... that's about it. I helped lots of people and within 12 months I was invited to become a sales director of my first company.

Since then I have owned and operated businesses in the UK and USA. I've taken them from start-up to stock market flotation. In each case I've been able to spot a niche and an opportunity, but most importantly - taken action on what I've seen. I'm driven by the thought of "what happens if I don't do it and someone else does..."

I helped grow my last UK IT business from scratch to over £32 million in annual revenues in just 8 years, becoming one of the "Times Top 100" fastest growing and profitable SME's in the country in the process. Again we niched. This time we created a proposition targeting IT related insurance claims rather than slog it out at retail.

In 2005 the company was sold and I was able to retire at the age of 45.

Since selling and taking early 'retirement' I'm busier than ever. I'm engaged by a number of 1-2-1 mentoring clients who want to take their business to the next level and turn to me for guidance and inspiration. I run a number of business mentoring groups for like-minded entrepreneurs and speak at seminars and conferences all around the world.

Over recent months I've been fortunate to have been paid to speak all across the UK and Europe as well as further afield in The Middle East, South Africa, Mexico, The USA, China, India, Australia, and New Zealand.

As speaker and presenter, I'm always wanting to capture video at events. So along with my business partner we've just created and launched a fantastic innovative little product called Hey Mic! The worlds' first Bluetooth lapel mic which links via my app to your smartphone.

Always driven and excited by a challenge; myself and another business partner have managed to secure the US licence for 20 years for an amazing patented 'clean tech' product. And so I'm off to California next to disrupt the trucking industry. We can save operators 25% in diesel consumption and reduce emissions by 35% too. Exciting times ahead.

Spot an opportunity - take action...

Here are several top tips I share with my audiences that I now share in the hope they may help you in your entrepreneurial journey too.

Knowledge isn't power

It's the application of knowledge that counts. I know plenty of very clever people who are broke. Know enough to feel confident and to inspire confidence and then allow people to buy from you.

Your success is very unlikely going to be down to a qualification you have.

Surround yourself with positive people

The company you keep will have a direct impact on your results, choose the company you keep carefully. If you have negative people around you, don't walk away from them... RUN!

Be fit for purpose

Practice what you preach. If you sell diet pills please don't be 10 Kilos overweight. If you help people to stop smoking - please don't smoke.

Resist the attraction of distraction

Focus on the why and the how will come. Don't get distracted by all the 'stuff'. Focus on three things each day that will move you towards your goal and set 90 minutes aside to work on these things and these things alone. No other email, no mobiles, no Facebook. WTF... Where's The Focus.

Get out of your comfort zone

Get into your stretch zone to see the best results. Nothing great happens in your comfort zone.

Don't live in the past

"The past is for reference, not for residence" Learn to let go and move on. What's done is done, you can't change it. Always look forwards and keep an eye on the prize.

Take the seven day challenge

Ready for this... Seven days of no complaining. Not about the kids, clients, work colleagues. Not about your husband or wife. When you develop a new habit of no complaining, you'll be amazed at the results you see.

Best of luck on your journey.

STEVE CLARKE
www.eurekaselling.co.uk
www.loveheymic.com
www.addvantage.net

EILEEN MORRISON

Beautiful Bea

www.beautifulbea.com

Beautiful Bea

If someone had told me ten months ago that I would be taking a career break from my job as a Police Officer to become a stay-at-home mum and sell natural skincare whilst juggling a blog and Vlog, I would have laughed.

But here I am; two and a half years after changing my cosmetics to Tropic Skincare, actually selling the products to a very loyal customer base, nurturing my own team of twelve amazing ladies and developing my website - beautifulbea.com with my own blog and YouTube Channel.

It all began in early 2015 when my good friend started selling Tropic Skincare after retiring as a Police Officer. She asked me to host a pamper party at mine so she could grow her customer base further than where she lived. I just love the idea of any form of pampering and was only too happy to oblige. I fell in love instantly with the products. I was at a difficult stage in my life as I had suffered multiple miscarriages and my skin was showing signs of classic hormonal outbreaks. I was also desperate to eliminate any form of chemicals that I was putting into my body. My skin had never looked and felt better once I switched to only natural products.

I was always telling family and friends about how much I loved the products and the ethos behind completely natural and fresh skincare. It felt like the most natural decision to join as an ambassador in November 2016.

Go do it!

My main reason was to get the discount (25%) and to use the opportunity as a social event as I was feeling a little like I'd lost some of my identity from becoming a mum. I joined at an incredibly stressful time as I had just gone back to work after a year off on maternity leave; my daughter was only 9 months old and between my shifts at work and my husbands, there was very little time to do anything other than my day job and care for my daughter.

I knew within 5 weeks (just before Christmas 2016) that it was going to be much bigger than what I had initially anticipated. I couldn't get out in the traditional sense and do pamper parties/events due to childcare, I was reliant on friends and friends of friends coming into my home for what I like to call 1-2-1 chats, demonstrations and where I couldn't pull people into my home, I would send out little baskets of products so potential customers could trial them in the comfort of their own home.

By chance one evening I did a Facebook Live on my Tropic Page to talk about why I joined and how I felt about my future with Tropic. It was a game changing moment for me. I sounded so nervous and I had a wobble in my voice but as soon as I looked down and saw the names of people (particularly strangers) tuning in to listen to me I just relaxed into it. I realised the power of connecting with my customers via live videos. It was my love of doing Facebook lives - doing demonstrations, general chats and competitions, that lead to me creating my YouTube Channel.

Against all the odds I slowly built a large and extremely loyal customer base and made the decision to join a local business group at the strong recommendation of my good friend - Danielle Durrant (thecobbledkitchen.co.uk)

I was hesitant in joining as although it was a small fee, I couldn't see how other business owners were going to benefit me and also I just assumed that I wouldn't be able to bring anything into the group. Oh the irony is not lost on me on just how wrong I was. The very best decision I made for my business was joining St Albans Business group SAB!

The amount of support, help, encouragement and not forgetting the friendships I have already formed have boosted me and benefited my business so much that I look forward to connecting with this group on a daily basis. I was so foolish and naive to not see the importance of networking in a business sense. I feel so much a part of a huge community where we are all behind and beside each other.

The second best decision I made was having a website (designed by an amazingly talented lady-DigitalJen.co.uk) where I could post my blogs (about Tropic and people I have met in the SAB group) and eventually my YouTube Channel Vlogs. It goes without saying that this group would not even exist or operate in the way it does without our inspiring mentor - Sue Wybrow. She is a force and a huge ball of energy!

I am so excited and full of anticipation for what the rest of my journey holds. I've only just got started!

EILEEN MORRISON
www.beautifulbea.com

Go do it!